A WORLD OF COSTUME AND TEXTILES

A World of Costume and Textiles

A HANDBOOK OF THE COLLECTION

EDITED BY SUSAN ANDERSON HAY

MUSEUM OF ART

RHODE ISLAND SCHOOL OF DESIGN

PROVIDENCE, RHODE ISLAND

1988

List of Authors

VIRGINIA BARRETT

MAGGIE BICKFORD

EDWARD DWYER

ELIZABETH ENCK

ANNE W. FISCHER

THIERRY GENTIS

SUSAN ANDERSON HAY

THOMAS LENTZ

JANE INGLE OHLY

PAMELA A. PARMAL

ROBIN PRESS

MADELYN SHAW

JOYCE SMITH

Museum Editor: Bianca K. Gray

This catalogue has been made possible by generous grants from the National Endowment for the Arts, a Federal agency, and from the Wm. H. Harris Co. in honor of its 80th anniversary.

©Rhode Island School of Design, 1988

Library of Congress
Catalogue Card No. 88-061499
ISBN 0-911517-51-0

COVER:
Flemish, Tournai, ca. 1520
Grand Verdure Tapestry with Animals (detail)
Wool (catalogue no. 51)

FRONTISPIECE:
Japanese, 19th century
Stencil (detail)
Mulberry paper, persimmon tannin (catalogue no. 45)

Table of Contents

Acknowledgments

A project of this magnitude is never completed without the help of many people, and we gratefully extend our thanks to every person who contributed to this handbook.

First and foremost, we recognize the generous contributions of the donors to this Museum, who gave the beautiful works illustrated in this volume. Without discerning donors, no collection could exist at all, and to them we owe the pleasure of working with such important examples of the weaver's art.

Co-authors Virginia Barrett, Maggie Bickford, Edward Dwyer, Elizabeth Enck, Anne W. Fischer, Thierry Gentis, Thomas Lentz, Jane Ingle Ohly, Robin Press, Madelyn Shaw, and Joyce Smith, contributed their indispensable services in their particular areas of expertise; to them we are especially grateful.

Others who helped us with expertise were Carol M. Spawn, Academy of Natural Sciences, Philadelphia; Cynthia Cannon, Art Institute of Chicago; Penelope Byrde, Museum of Costume, Bath, England; Ann Morse and Jean-Michel Tuchscherer, Museum of Fine Arts, Boston; Ann Coleman, Brooklyn Museum; Gillian Moss and Milton Sonday, Cooper-Hewitt Museum, New York; Aileen Ribiero, Courtauld Institute of Art, London; Betty Kirke and Shirley Eng, Fashion Institute of Technology, New York; Robert L. Welsch, Field Museum of Natural History, Chicago; Barbara Hail and Margot Schevill, Haffenreffer Museum of Anthropology, Brown University, Bristol, Rhode Island; Monni Adams, Harvard University, Cambridge, Massachusetts; Elizabeth Jarvis, Peter Parker and Ellen Ramsey, Historical Society of Pennsylvania, Philadelphia; Jane Kolter, Independence National Historical Park, Philadelphia; Dale Gluckman and Sharon Takeda, Los Angeles County Museum of Art; Deborah Brown, Jean Druesedow and Michelle Majer, Metropolitan Museum of Art, New York; Monique Drosson and Jacqueline Jacqué, Musée de l'Impression sur Etoffes, Mulhouse, France; Pierre Arrizoli-Clementel and Monique Jay, Musée Historique des Tissus, Lyon; Mme Josette Brédif, Musée Oberkampf, Jouy-en-Josas, France; Dilys Blum, Monica Brown, Felice Fischer, and Barbara Sevy, Philadelphia Museum of Art; Paul Bourcier, Rhode Island Historical Society; Eleanor H. Smith, Richmond Historical Society, Richmond, Rhode Island; Scott Redford, Sackler Museum, Harvard University, Cambridge, Massachusetts; Philip L. Ravenhill, National Museum of African Art, Smithsonian Institution, Washington, D.C.; Iwao Nagasaki, Tokyo National Museum, Japan; Anna Gonosová, University of California, Irvine; Susan Swan and Neville Thompson, H. F. DuPont Winterthur Museum, Winterthur, Delaware; and Santina Levy and Natalie Rothstein, Victoria and Albert Museum, London. Judith Applegate, New York; Adolph Cavallo, New York; Marie Jo de Chaignon, Lyon, France; Cora Ginsburg and Titi Halle, New York; Pat Griffiths, Amsterdam, Netherlands; Donald King, London; Roberta Landini, Florence, Italy; Marguerite Prinet, Paris; Marjorie Schunke, West Kingston, Rhode Island; and Margaret Swain, Edinburgh, Scotland, were also especially helpful. Junichi Arai, with Elaine Lipton as translator, and Cynthia Schira generously shared information about themselves and their work. Ann Morse, Boston Museum of Fine Arts, kindly translated hundreds of notes by Iwao Nagasaki on the RISD collection from the Japanese. Sarah Lederberg did important preliminary research on French fashion designers. John Anderson, Chairman, Department of Anthropology, Brown University, lent us a microscope for weave analysis, necessary to our undertaking. We wish to offer our special thanks to Elliott Brodsky and Armand Versaci, whose gift of a microscope for fiber analysis was basic to our technical analyses.

We wish also to thank the staffs of the libraries we consulted at Brown University; the Costume Institute of the Metropolitan Museum of Art; the New York Public Library; the Philadelphia Museum of Art; the Pierpont Morgan Library, New York; The University of Illinois, Champaign; The University Museum, Philadelphia; the University of Pennsylvania; the University of Rhode Island; the Watson Library at the Metropolitan Museum of Art, New York; and the H. F. DuPont Winterthur Museum.

At the Rhode Island School of Design, we acknowledge the help of Matthew J. Alaimo, Jr., Laurie Averill, and Carol Terry in the Library; and in the Museum, Cynthea Bogel, Linda Catano, Madeleine Cody, Melody Ennis, Florence Friedman, Thomas Michie, Christopher Monkhouse, Daniel Rosenfeld, David Stark, Jean Waterman, and Carla Woodward. Former Curator of the Aldrich Collection Elizabeth T. Casey gave us important information on the collection and identified photographs of Lucy Truman Aldrich, and Eleanor Fayerweather shared her many recollections of RISD and the Museum during her tenure as Curator. Edward Dwyer of the School reviewed the Peruvian textile entries, and James Trilling contributed essential expertise in the entries for Coptic textiles.

In the Museum, we would like to thank Director Frank Robinson, who lent his support and expertise at every stage of the project. We owe a great debt to Assistant Director, Kathleen Bayard, who shepherded the project through every stage, from writing grant applications to organizing its production. Bianca Gray was indispensable as editor of this publication; and Janet Phillips Rushton contributed editorial advice. Ethel Rudy of the Haffenreffer Museum of Anthropology, Bristol, Rhode Island, contributed her clerical services. We warmly acknowledge the contributions of Marsha Cain, who patiently carried out the typing and endless correction of this manuscript. The services of Lora Urbanelli and William Rae, and their expertise in preparing the manuscript for publication, can only be suggested here.

Robert Thornton, the Museum photographer, undertook the difficult task of photographing the objects here reproduced; textiles, and particularly costume, are among the most difficult museum objects to photograph because of their visual complexity. To him we owe a special expression of gratitude. Gilbert Associates, particularly Joseph and Melissa Gilbert, devoted their talents to the production of this handsome book.

Finally, we wish to thank the National Endowment for the Arts, a Federal agency, and Wm. H. Harris Co., for the essential support without which this publication would not have been possible.

S.A.H. and P.P.

COLLECTORS AND CURATORS
A History of the Collection

When Helen Metcalf and her trustees founded RISD in 1877, the by-laws they wrote included these specific aims: instruction in drawing and design so that students could "apply the principles of art to the requirements of trade and manufacture," and systematic training in the principles of art in order to "give instruction to others and become artists," were to be combined with "the collection and exhibition of works of art."[1]

Although the study of textiles was not at first included, it was envisaged from the first. An informal plan of operations dated March 23, 1877, held that "instruction... may be extended... although not at present... [to] the application of designing to the useful arts, as, for example, to designing for calico prints, for weaving, for jewelers designs... and for other uses."[2]

Although the School was at first unable to take on such a large program, it was no surprise that textiles were in the minds of the founders. Helen Metcalf was the wife of Jesse Metcalf, the owner of woolen mills at Wanskuck, in Providence, a man not without an interest in hoping for better design for weaving. Moreover, others who were founding museums and art schools in America after the Centennial Exposition planned textile design as one of the subjects, acknowledging that the United States had to encourage its own students to overcome the European superiority in design that was all too evident in Centennial exhibits. These included the founders of the Philadelphia Museum and School, no doubt known to the Rhode Island women, who championed the example of the Victoria and Albert Museum where textiles were collected from the very first.

The first attempt to teach textile design at RISD occurred almost immediately, when in 1880 and 1881 some of the most popular classes were those in art needlework. By 1887, the promise that "collection and exhibition" would be part of RISD's mission was also being dealt with.

ELIZA RADEKE AND THE FOUNDING OF THE TEXTILE COLLECTION

A small industrial collection had been started immediately with models for technical drawing, casts and bas-reliefs, and in 1887, "gifts of textiles" were added to a collection of implements brought from Germany in 1885. Dr. Gustav Radeke, the son-in-law of Jesse and Helen Metcalf, had taken an interest in the Museum since the founding of the School, and as a wealthy physician with connections in Germany, he could discover and import some of the tools used in art education there. Together he and his wife Eliza were the first great supporters of the Museum, and it is probably from them that the "gifts of textiles" came.

1. Carla Mathes Woodward and Franklin W. Robinson, eds., *A Handbook of the Museum of Art, Rhode Island School of Design*, Providence, Rhode Island, Rhode Island School of Design, 1985, hereafter cited as *Handbook*, p. 11.

2. Quoted in Elsie S. Bronson, "The Rhode Island School of Design: A Half-Century Record (1878–1928)," typescript, RISD Archives.

When Dr. Radeke died in 1892, the notion of the "industrial museum" seems to have vanished with him. But the art museum, under the guidance of Mrs. Radeke, took its place, actually beginning to collect in 1891, and it was Mrs. Radeke who essentially established the textile collection by making a number of donations in 1901.

Elizabeth Greene Metcalf Radeke was a remarkable person. Born in Georgia in 1854, where her father was a cotton agent for New England mills, Eliza Metcalf was one of the early students at Vassar College, graduating in 1876.[3] After graduation she accompanied her mother to the Centennial Exposition in Philadelphia, where she served as a hostess in the Rhode Island Building, the source of the $1675.00 with which her mother founded RISD.[4]

In 1880 she married Gustav Radeke, immediately beginning to collect textiles as well as other objects, with the Museum in mind. After the idea of the industrial museum began to wither, the Radekes kept up their donations to the art museum, making the first donations of tapa cloth, American Indian moccasins, and a Siamese fan to the textile collection in 1891. In 1892, when Dr. Radeke died, his wife saw only two objects acquired for the Museum, both textiles: a costume from the "Feejee" islands and a piece of tapa cloth given by Mrs. Sidney Clementson.

For the rest of the century, while the first museum building took shape, no textiles were acquired. Two textile exhibitions did take place, however, in 1899 in the new Waterman Building, a loan exhibition of Persian embroideries and a second exhibition of Japanese embroideries. In 1900 came an exhibition of embroidery lent by Miss Louisa D. Sharpe. The tradition of exhibiting textiles was thus firmly established, not to be interrupted to this day.

In 1901, Mrs. Radeke began the first of many donations of historical textiles. Of the 29 objects given to the Museum that year, she gave eight to the textile collection, all Italian vestments. In other years she gave to the collection Kashmir shawls, sewing implements, beaded bags, and other objects, but her interest seemed primarily to be in Japanese textiles, of which she gave several collections of brocaded fabrics. In 1905 and 1907 she established with two substantial donations the Museum's considerable collection of Japanese stencils (cat. no. 45), and a collection of sample books of Japanese textiles that is unique outside Japan. Taking a hands-on approach to her involvement with the Museum, she concerned herself in 1907 with purchasing a textile case, table, and lighting for a new textile study room. This personal interest in the care of the textiles and their use by the students of the newly formed division of textile design, together with her continuing donations, marked the career of this committed and discerning leader, President of RISD between 1913 and 1918, and strong supporter of the textile collection until her death in 1931. Her sense of commitment was the driving force behind the emergence in the following years of the collection as a distinguished part of both School and Museum.

Meanwhile, the Museum was reaching out to the community as well as the School. In 1915, the year of the completion of the Metcalf textile building for the Textile School, it held a loan exhibition of printed textiles, Rhode Island samplers, and portraits in collaboration with Brown University to celebrate the 150th anniversary of Brown. Reflecting the revival of interest in the American colonial period that began in the last years of the 19th century and found expression at RISD in 1906 with the opening of Pendleton House as the first

3. *Who's Who In New England*, 2nd ed., Boston, 1919, in which she was one of the few women mentioned.

4. *Handbook*, p. 11.

In 1902, the Museum held an exhibition of Japanese porcelains, screens, bronzes, and textiles in the Waterman building

American wing in any museum, it inspired an influx of textile donations newly oriented towards American history. Early American needlework appeared on the accession lists; the first American quilts and coverlets were acquired. Susan Thurston gave Rhode Island samplers and embroideries, Mrs. H. T. Brown gave printed textiles and a documented handkerchief brought to this country from England in 1787, and Miss Mary Anne Greene gave needlework and fans. Many years later, thanks to these beginnings, the Museum has a collection of New England needlework of great rarity, and a collection beyond compare of school-girl samplers made at the Balch School in Providence.

Thanks to the efforts of many donors, including Mrs. Radeke, Lyra Brown Nickerson, Louisa D. Sharpe (later Mrs. Jesse H. Metcalf), and Mrs. E. M. Arnold in particular, the Museum had by this time accumulated a collection of European silks, Persian silks, vestments and embroideries, enough to attract attention outside of Providence. In 1915, Dr. E. Meyer Riefstahl asked the Museum to lend a number of "valuable examples to the Historical Exhibit of Textiles. This was held at the time of the First National Silk Convention in Paterson, New Jersey, October 12 to 31."[5] The Museum was one of only six lenders, an indication of its importance already at that early date.

Matters of interest to the School were not neglected; in addition to purchases of lace, and brocaded and printed textile samples for study, donations of Indian artifacts, Japanese textiles, and contemporary American silk weavings arrived in the Museum. Exhibitions of modern silks, Persian brocades, Chinese embroideries, textile and wallpaper designs from the Art Alliance of America, and textile exhibitions circulated by the American Federation of the Arts were among those hung in the Waterman Building galleries before 1921.

Acknowledging this progress in 1923, the *Providence Magazine* declared, "The most distinctive thing about the Rhode Island School of Design as a whole is the close cooperation of its departments of Fine and Applied Arts with its Museum,... classes are constantly being taken into the Museum for informal talks on the collections; much drawing and research work is done in all its departments,... [and] the constant acquisitions to the Museum are made with the School's needs in view, particularly in regard to jewelry and textiles."[6]

5. Minutes of the Museum Committee, December 7, 1915.

6. Typescript, RISD Archives.

To oversee all this activity, Mrs. Radeke in 1912 had appointed L. Earle Rowe as Director of the School, and in this capacity he also acted as Director of the Museum. A classicist by training, his interests did not stop at Greece and Rome, but extended to Egypt, from which he acquired many fine works, including the collection's first Coptic textiles. European, Persian, Japanese and ancient Peruvian artifacts (among many others) were also acquired in volume during his tenure, and he saw to it that many textiles were among them. In 1921 he hired an assistant, later named curator, Miriam A. Banks. Also a classicist, she was a perfect foil for Rowe, specializing in areas in which he did not, and her interest in tapestries and in needlework helped to shape the collection during the following decades of great growth.

In 1918 under Rowe's aegis, the Museum made its first textile purchase, a 17th century Persian brocade purchased from K. Minassian of New York for $100. A second purchase of Persian textiles on October 16, 1918, was made from Moustapha Avigdor, a Persian whose collection had been displayed at the Museum earlier that year.

During the next ten years, purchases of tapestries were high on the agenda. The Museum had already acquired a Gothic tapestry fragment, and in 1926 Rowe bought a small millefleurs tapestry from P. W. French and Company, New York, for $5060, a large sum for the day. In 1927 the Museum purchased a fragment of a tapestry of scenes from the Wars of Troy, and two Tournai verdure tapestries. In 1929 came a beautiful fragment depicting a hunting scene with falcon, and in 1930 an important armorial tapestry with the coat of arms of the Duke of Beaufort, thus creating a small but choice collection of Gothic tapestries.

In 1931, Eliza Metcalf Radeke died. In spite of the loss of this great supporter of textiles, Rowe continued his enthusiasm for this part of the collection.

The textile study room in the late 1920s

The year 1931 saw the textile collection well advanced, and in 1933 the Museum Committee took a step that ensured its permanent excellence, appointing to a vacancy caused by the death of Dorothy Sturgis, Miss Lucy Truman Aldrich. A collector of European porcelain and Asian and American decorative arts, Miss Aldrich also had an exquisite collection of Asian silks. In the twenty years remaining before her death she became the single greatest donor to the RISD textile collection.

Lucy Truman Aldrich, born in Providence in 1869, was the oldest daughter of banker Nelson W. Aldrich, then a Republican member of the Providence Common Council and a future United States Senator (1881-1911). She grew up in the Aldrich house at 110 Benevolent Street (and indeed lived there the rest of her life), which her father's growing wealth enabled him to furnish with beautiful objects, paintings, and a splendid library. Educated at Miss Porter's in Farmington, Connecticut, she was particularly close to her sister Abby, who married John D. Rockefeller, Jr. in 1901. Before Abby's marriage, the sisters traveled together in Europe admiring art galleries and museums, each developing eventually an irresistible urge to collect. "To me art is one of the great resources of my life," wrote Mrs. Rockefeller in 1929 before giving the first of many paintings to the Museum of Modern Art, which she helped to found.[7] Her sister Lucy shared this opinion, beginning early to collect prints, furniture, and textiles, which she said she especially loved because of their color and texture. Abby Aldrich Rockefeller began her important collection of Japanese prints in the first years of the century, and it was she who introduced her sister to the Orient, where Lucy ventured for the first time in 1919.

In Yokohama, at her sister's instigation, Miss Aldrich visited Yamanaka and Company, a firm which, in addition to the prints purchased by Mrs. Rockefeller, sold old Japanese silks and priest's robes. The brocades she purchased there in May of 1919 were her first Oriental textiles and the foundation of her extensive collection. Yamanaka, with offices in New York, Boston and Bar Harbor, as well as the main cities of Japan, remained her main source for many years. After their sojourn in Japan, Miss Aldrich and an entourage which included her niece Babs Rockefeller, spent a month in Peking, where they borrowed the house of a Consular official. Here the conversion of Miss Aldrich to Oriental textiles became complete. To the house came Chinese textile merchants, particularly one called "Big Li." Big Li, reported the *Providence Journal* after an interview with Miss Aldrich in 1938, "would hold each piece in the best light, enjoying himself the beauty for which he was going to get the best price possible."[8] From him Miss Aldrich bought Chinese priests' robes, Ch'ing dynasty imperial costumes, embroidered sleeve bands, mandarin squares, and other textiles.

This first trip to Asia concluded with stops in India, Ceylon, and Burma. Aldrich records do not indicate whether textile purchases were made during these sojourns, although Miss Aldrich's letters to her sister Abby recount her enjoyment in the exotic places and unexpected events of Indian travel.

But Miss Aldrich's best travel stories were reserved for her next trip, to China, in 1923, and were told and retold by her in letters, newspapers, and in an article in *Atlantic Monthly*. High-spirited and adventurous despite congenital deafness, Miss Aldrich always took a companion with her when she traveled, usually Miss Minnie A. McFadden, who oversaw the household at

Lucy Truman Aldrich (right), with Minnie McFadden (center) on a trip to India in 1920–1921

7. Quoted in Mary Ellen Chase, *Abby Aldrich Rockefeller*, New York, Macmillan, 1950, p. 130.

8. *Providence Journal*, March 6, 1938.

Miss Aldrich in Peking

110 Benevolent Street. In May of 1923 she and Miss McFadden were on their way by train to Peking when the train was stopped and robbed at 2:30 a.m. by bandits. The two women, in their nightgowns and slippers, were herded down the track together with other Westerners and some Chinese passengers for a distance that took the rest of the night to walk. Separated from Miss McFadden after the bandits shot to death an uncooperative passenger, Miss Aldrich was freed mysteriously and suddenly in the middle of the countryside, where friendly villagers rescued her, and took her to a larger town where she was reunited with Miss McFadden and others in her party.[9] Long after the incident, the Chinese government paid reparations to the travelers, a sum Lucy Truman Aldrich characteristically spent on further purchases of Chinese textiles for her collection.

From this time on, perhaps understandably, her attention turned to Japan. By 1925 she had established a close relationship with Yamanaka and Company in Kyoto, where in August of that year she purchased "29 pieces of Old Japanese 'No' dance costumes" and "1 piece of ditto costume" for 24,242 yen, the equivalent of $10,000.[10] The Noh robe collection thus begun encompassed Miss Aldrich's finest Asian textiles, finer even than her Ch'ing Dynasty costumes acquired in Peking. Fortunately, Yamanaka and Company were interested in and proud of the provenance of the Noh robes they sold. On the paper wrappers they supplied with each textile, they wrote the information they knew, including dates, actor's parts and names, and the name of the Japanese court at which each robe had been specially made for Noh play productions. This information, together with the range of dates and types of robes and the even, fine quality of all the pieces, makes her collection unique, one of the finest outside Japan.

9. Lloyd Lehrbas, *China Press*, May 10, 1923, typescript, Aldrich Papers, Rhode Island Historical Society (hereafter cited as RIHS).

10. Bill, August 2, 1925, Aldrich Papers, RIHS.

When in 1933 Miss Aldrich became part of the Museum Committee, she had the precedent of her sister's involvement with the Museum of Modern Art in New York. Not one of the original founders of the Museum, but head of the essential committee that raised the first millions for endowment, Abby Aldrich Rockefeller cared deeply about the Museum of Modern Art and gradually donated many of the modernist paintings she had been collecting since the early 1920s.

True to this inspiration and precedent, the following year Lucy Truman Aldrich gave to the RISD Museum her collection of embroidered Chinese sleeve bands and other Chinese embroidery, lending to the Museum her extensive collection of Indian, Persian, Turkish, and Greek Island textiles. In addition, she persuaded her sister to give to RISD the collection of Japanese prints she had been developing since early in the century by purchase in Japan and New York.

Miss Aldrich also gave her collection of European porcelains, together with a plan to build a room especially for them. This largesse was accepted joyfully "with an expression of the delight of the Committee in the great enrichment of the museum, especially in the field of decorative arts," and plans began immediately to be made for the display of the porcelains.[11]   The great collection of Noh robes, however, was scheduled in 1935 to be shown at the Metropolitan Museum of Art in an exhibition organized by the Metropolitan's curator of Asian art, Alan Priest, one of the first showings of Noh robes in this country. Twelve of the Aldrich robes were shown in the exhibition, and were valued in January of 1935 by Yamanaka for insurance purposes at $13,300. When compared to the robes Dr. Priest borrowed from Japan, the Aldrich robes were "very fine," and when it came to the "eight or ten robes belonging to the [Metropolitan] museum," Yamanaka declared that "none of these can compare with yours."[12] After the exhibition, at the end of April, Miss Aldrich, in Europe all year, had the robes sent to Providence, where they were welcomed gratefully by her old friend and new RISD president Helen Danforth.

Abby Aldrich Rockefeller and Helen Danforth together oversaw the plans for the proposed porcelain room in Miss Aldrich's absence during 1935. The porcelains eventually took their place in specially designed cabinets in a room paneled with 18th century carved woodwork from Chipstead Place in England, donated by the two sisters and Helen Danforth.

When it came to installation and storage of the pieces she gave, Miss Aldrich set a precedent she insisted upon in future years: only she was allowed to install her collection, or persons she specifically designated. In 1935 she and Miss McFadden made the arrangement of the porcelains. Miss Aldrich later came to trust the young assistant, Elizabeth T. Casey, who had been appointed by Earle Rowe, and only she of the museum staff was allowed to handle the Noh robe collection. Again Miss Aldrich kept close supervision, providing wooden cases for the storage of the robes, and insisting on the placement of tiny specially made cushions between the folds and bits of camphor in the corners of the cases to keep out moths.

Although much of her time in the 1930s was spent abroad, when she was in Providence Miss Aldrich did not neglect the Museum. In 1937 she sent Japanese tassels, Indian painted cottons, and a gold-encrusted sari, and appeared in person to install the opening exhibition of her Japanese priests' robes, held in the Main Gallery, April 6 to May 10, 1937. The Noh robes were installed in

11. Minutes of Museum Committee,
    December 11, 1934.

12. Letter, Boston, Mass., January 17, 1935,
    Aldrich Papers, RIHS.

"Kesa from the Lucy Truman Aldrich
Collection," 1937

The Lucy Truman Aldrich Collection of Noh
robes on display in the "Silk Room," 1937

the Silk Room in limed oak cases, especially designed in 1936 by Nakagawa
of Boston, and were hung on rods suspended from the tops of the cases.

Throughout the years 1938 to 1940, Lucy Truman Aldrich remained the
mainstay of the exhibition program as well as the collection, thanks to the
construction of these cases meant exclusively for the exhibition of textiles from
her collection. In 1938 the Museum mounted an exhibition of her Chinese
costumes in the upper galleries on E floor. In June 1939 she lent Indian textiles
for display, and later in the year works from the Dutch East Indies. In 1940
three different selections from her collection in the Museum were shown,
including Chinese costumes, East Indian costumes, and "oriental costume."
She continued to insist that only she could unlock the storage cases and install
the costumes; she did this with Elizabeth Casey until the latter's departure in
1942, after which Miss Aldrich's interest seems to have flagged.

Miss Aldrich apparently did not come often to the Museum during the
war years, and by 1947 was surprised to find that the room where her textiles
had been displayed in 1938 was no longer being devoted solely to the Aldrich
collection. Moreover, Abby Aldrich Rockefeller's Japanese prints were not
always on display in the adjacent rooms. The issue became even more acute
when Abby died suddenly in 1949. Talking things over first with John D.
Rockefeller, Jr., and Helen Danforth, Miss Aldrich enlisted Abby's sons Nelson
and David to help her develop a plan for new rooms to be dedicated to the
memory of Abby Aldrich Rockefeller, including a new version of her "Silk
Room." Miss Aldrich hired the young architect Philip Johnson, then head of
the Architecture Department at the Museum of Modern Art, to design the
room for Abby's prints, while William G. Perry oversaw the renovation and
reinstallation of the textile gallery.

During the project the modest $3,000 Miss Aldrich had considered giving in
1949 increased considerably. Special lighting was installed, and benches were
designed by Johnson himself. The Porcelain Gallery was restored and a new
bridge built into Pendleton House to relieve traffic. In all, the cost of the project
to the Rockefeller family by 1952 was $17,778.66 for what all agreed were five
wonderful new rooms.[13] At the opening of the rooms in 1953, Miss Aldrich

13. Letter, William Edwards to Lucy Truman
    Aldrich, December 2, 1952, Aldrich Papers,
    RIHS.

spoke a few words, expressing her delight that the Asian silks were again on display and that Elizabeth T. Casey would be their permanent curator, appointed at her insistence Keeper of the Aldrich Collection and Curator of Oriental Art.

Reassured about the safety of the Museum as a repository of her works of art, she deposited at the Museum in 1953 and 1954 most of her remaining textiles. Even so, when she died in 1954, a great number remained in her estate. Many of these were bequeathed to the Museum; others were donated in the following few years by her heirs, her nephews Nelson, Laurance, and David Rockefeller.

ALEXANDER DORNER: AN EMPHASIS ON "APPLIED ARTS"

In 1937, the Museum's first and so far, only Director, Earl Rowe, had died. The appointment of Dr. Alexander Dorner, former Director of the Landesmuseum in Hannover, Germany, and a refugee from Hitler, inaugurated a new era for the Museum. Dorner reemphasized the connection of the Museum with the School, and called on the Museum to make "no separation . . . between fine . . . and . . . applied arts," including textiles.[14] He called for more examples of "applied arts" to be acquired, setting in motion a program of purchases that lasted until the 1950s. Although the approach of war somewhat hampered these efforts, he was able to obtain a donation from the medieval enthusiast and collector of armor, Carl Otto von Kienbusch, of medieval and Renaissance textiles, and to purchase several important Coptic and Peruvian textiles. His greatest achievement for the textile collection, however, was the purchase of the famous Napoleonic lace "couverture" that had been made for the Empress Josephine but presented to Marie Louise (cat. no. 73), an addition that complemented the earlier donation by Mrs. Harold Brown of a distinguished collection of Napoleonic furnishings and other objects, itself the subject of an exhibition in 1941.

The exhibition of textiles also prospered under Dorner; before his resignation in 1941 at least 18 exhibitions devoted wholly to textiles or including textiles in their subject matter were held, including the many based on the Aldrich collection, together with French printed cottons, Turkish and Italian textiles, Coptic textiles, Indian and Paisley shawls, and two exhibitions of tapestries.

The Museum's Gobelins tapestry (cat. no. 56) on display shortly after its acquisition in 1937

RUDOLF BERLINER: THE CURATOR AS TEXTILE SPECIALIST

Throughout the 1920s and 1930s, Miriam Banks had served as curator of everything, including textiles, ably assisted by Elizabeth T. Casey, her sister Dorothy, and others. Gordon Washburn, who became director in 1941, expanded the staff by appointing another German refugee, Heinrich Schwarz, to oversee paintings, sculpture, and prints. In 1942 he appointed Dr. Rudolf Berliner Curator of Decorative Arts. Berliner, also a refugee, from a museum background in Munich and recently a curator at the Cooper Union in New York, enthusiastically expanded the textile collection, and in fact, seemed to specialize in textiles, purchasing thousands of examples for the Museum before his retirement in 1952. During his curatorship textiles poured in, by gift as well as purchase, including quilts, tapestries, lace, printed textiles, Rhode Island 18th century costume, and a large group of Polynesian textiles collected by the Governor of American Samoa in the 1920s (cat. no. 34).

14. *Handbook*, p. 41.

By purchase came Spanish lampas, Utrecht velvets, Turkish textiles, two chasubles, a collection of Fortuny fabrics, and several embroideries, from early 1946 to mid-1947 alone. A breakdown of expenditures for works of art purchased by the Museum Committee on February 10, 1947 showed prints and drawings to have cost $925, ceramics $963, numismatics $1,000, wooden objects $380, and textiles, $1,340. Berliner explained his purchasing philosophy to the Committee by saying he wanted to "fill in the gaps in the Museum's collection and to enable students to trace the development of designs." He explained "that the textile students used not only textiles to study designs, but also other decorative arts objects [and] mentioned that students of Interior Design, Art History, Textile Design, Costume Design, Ceramics, and Sculpture make use of the textile study rooms."[15]

Berliner was interested in contemporary textiles as well as historic examples, feeling that it was essential for students to see the best work of the moment. In an exhibition in early 1947 called "Textile Panorama," prepared in collaboration with the Brooklyn Museum, he undertook to show not only examples of historic textiles, but the best designs of British and American companies such as Ascher and Company, Schumacher, Dan Cooper, Onondaga, Cohn-Hall-Marx, and Leslie Tillett. After the exhibition, each company donated the samples it had sent, creating what today is an important corpus of early screen-printed textiles for study.

Another of Berliner's textile exhibitions took place in 1949, called "Men and Animals in Textile Arts," using long-held textiles and newly-acquired objects like the Safavid silk with horse and rider (cat. no. 18). While he was preparing this exhibition the Museum received the largest textile gift in its history. Hundreds of sample books dating mostly from the end of the 19th and early 20th centuries, from the recently closed Arnold Print Works in North Adams, Massachusetts, were given by Jacob Ziskind, an incredibly valuable resource for the study of textiles in that period. The Museum Committee welcomed this donation for a reason of its own: its members were hoping to establish closer relations between the School, the Museum, and contemporary textile designers. "It was the sense of the Committee that the Ziskind Collection offers an admirable opening for furthering cooperation between our Museum and textile designers," the Minutes read.[16]

Textile design student, about 1937

Students in apparel design, 1944

15. Minutes of the Museum Committee, November 4, 1947.

16. October 10, 1949.

The annual exhibition of works by students of textile and apparel design took place in the Waterman galleries in 1947

Berliner enlisted three volunteers to work on the Ziskind Collection, mounting and matting some of the larger loose pieces, and cataloguing the intact sample books so that they could be used by students. Because of space limitations and the consensus that the books would be more easily available there, most of the books were transferred to the Museum of American Textile History in North Andover, Massachusetts, with its fine scholarly staff and library. The Museum retains a large sample of volumes which may be consulted by students and scholars.

Thanks to the efforts of Rudolf Berliner, the Museum also acquired in the following few years a collection of silk samples from Guard Frères in Lyon, an extensive and comprehensive collection of prints and wovens from the 1920s and 1930s. Before his retirement in 1952, Berliner had added many more textiles that he purchased in Europe, in an effort to fill in the gaps in textiles of the periods before and after the Ziskind Collection.

By 1949 Berliner had been successful in obtaining new cases for the textile materials. A study room for textiles was set up "which contains a growing collection of textiles of all cultures and times, including our own, and which is available for study to anyone." But Berliner suggested that students not limit themselves to textiles; in a statement that mirrored the philosophy of the Museum at that time, he insisted, "We believe in the principle that the artistic problems are basically the same for all the arts and crafts and that it is highly desirable not to limit the sources of inspiration for students."[17]

In 1952, Berliner retired, having achieved great growth in the collection and overseen its development as a resource for students in all departments of the School. His emphasis on contemporary textiles as well as historic examples set a new direction for the collection, resulting in its importance today as a resource for study of 20th century textile arts.

17. Letter, Rudolf Berliner to Raymond Brush, January 10, 1949, RISD Museum Archives.

When in 1952 John Maxon became Director, succeeding Acting Director Roberta Alford, an art historian and textile donor (cat. no. 4) who had taken over from Washburn in 1949, the long career of Eleanor Fayerweather was just beginning. Born in Boston, trained at the New England College of Art, a veteran of the Brooklyn Museum Education staff, Miss Fayerweather would be in charge of the newly created RISD costume collection for more than 25 years. During her career, she saw the collection transformed from a small haphazard study collection in the School into a large and distinguished one housed in the Museum.

Eleanor Fayerweather arrived at RISD in 1947, where as Assistant Professor she was in charge of costume history in the Apparel Design department. A "Costume Research" collection consisted of a few items from various donors, and one of Miss Fayerweather's first moves was to ask for more donations. "There is no reason why Rhode Island should not have one of the best collections in the country. I am certainly going to make every effort," she wrote in the year of her arrival.[18]

That costume was coming out of its role as historical frivolity appealing only to antiquarians was demonstrated again when in 1949 and 1950 the Museum itself under the aegis of Rudolf Berliner showed some contemporary gowns borrowed from the Brooklyn Museum: "A Decade of Fashion Design by Charles James." By 1954, Director Maxon thought the "Costume Research" collection important enough to move it over to the Museum, where a new storage area was built for it on C floor, encompassing the previous textiles storeroom in the present storage and workrooms in addition to the space now occupied by the Print Room. Miss Fayerweather came along as part-time curator. The opening of the costume study and storage areas in the fall of 1955 inspired a new flood of donations, this time costume: historic, contemporary (including each year the three outstanding designs from the School), and ethnographic.

Exhibitions involving costume became more frequent in the 1950s as well. In 1955 an exhibition entitled "Living in Style" included costume, and "Victorian Decorative Arts" included costume and accessories. Decorative Arts Curator Graeme Keith's exhibition "The World of the Thirties" in 1956 included textiles by Dan Cooper and Ruth Reeves, and costume designs by Gontcharova from the Theatre Arts Collection at the New York Public Library. The 1958–1959 calendar included a small parasol and fan show and an exhibition of contemporary Italian fashion, which was enjoying a great renaissance in the 1950s.

By 1959 the costume collection had become one of the most popular collections in the Museum. In 1961, new Director David Carter gave the collection an official name, "Costume Center," and gave Eleanor Fayerweather the title of curator. In 1961 the first exhibitions produced entirely by the new curator were on display: "Fashion by Eric" celebrated the fashion artist who drew for *Vogue* in the 30s, 40s, and 50s, and "Fashion's Future in the Past" included some of the best donations to the collection, costumes from 1800–1961. Especially popular were the Jessie Franklin Turner dresses given by Helen Danforth, and the Charles James ballgowns given by Mrs. William Randolph Hearst, Jr. (cat. no. 109).

All the while, and still on a part-time basis, Miss Fayerweather continued to teach classes at the School, bringing students in to study the collection and also

Costumes from the Museum's collection in the Wetmore Room in "The World of the Thirties," 1956

"Fashion's Future in the Past" showed the growing costume collection as a resource for contemporary design, 1961

18. Letter, Eleanor Fayerweather to Miss Anna Shepard, October 27, 1947, RISD Museum Archives.

Andy Warhol's "Raid the Icebox" showed the Museum's collection of Native American textiles, 1970

dealing with classes from the University of Rhode Island and Southern Massachusetts University.

Donations continued to arrive on the Museum's doorstep, and by 1969 the collection had become a distinguished one, with donations not only from important society leaders like Mrs. C. Oliver Iselin and Mrs. Rodman A. de Heeren, but from other institutions. Thanks to Eleanor Fayerweather's connections in New York, the Brooklyn Museum, the Museum of the City of New York, and the Fashion Institute of Technology through Robert Riley "not only transferred examples from their own collections but introduced us to new sources."[19] As costume consultant for the Society for the Preservation of New England Antiquities, she was given a superb gift from that collection of interesting 19th century examples. The United States Rubber Company also contributed a gift of early examples of galoshes, rubber-soled shoes, and other rubber footwear.

Although officially textiles were still in the Decorative Arts Department, Miss Fayerweather had their de facto care. During the 1960s she prepared textiles for the public to see and assisted authors with examples of printed textiles and embroidery for publication. She catered to an interest in the sample books in the collection and inquiries about the mills that made them, still a perennial interest of students who use the Museum.

The big event in the Museum in 1970 was what was essentially a "happening" produced by Andy Warhol called "Raid the Icebox." The exhibition was conceived by John and Dominique de Menil of Houston, where the exhibition also appeared, and stemmed from their visit with new Director Daniel Robbins to "appalling, stuffed storage," where they found Old Master drawings in dark cubicles obstructed by large paintings.[20] When Warhol came to Providence, the first object he demanded for his exhibition was the shoe cabinet, which he displayed in its entirety, with each shoe in it exhaustively described in the catalogue.

19. Report, Eleanor Fayerweather to Diana Johnson, Chief Curator, undated: probably 1974, RISD Museum Archives.

20. Daniel Robbins, "Confessions of a Museum Director," in *Raid the Icebox, with Andy Warhol*, Providence, Rhode Island, Rhode Island School of Design, 1969, pp. 8–15.

Less controversial exhibitions continued throughout the 1970s, including "Mountain Artisans" (1970), Miss Fayerweather's selection of quilts from contemporary Appalachia, and "Ceremonial Costumes" (1974), a selection of costumes "for public occasions," including Japanese court kimonos and the Napoleonic Court train. In 1979 Miss Fayerweather's most popular costume exhibition, "Costumes in Context," included paintings and decorative arts objects.

1980–1988: THE COSTUME AND TEXTILE COLLECTION COMBINED AND FLOURISHING

Since 1980 costume and textile exhibitions have continued, including "New England Samplers" and "Japanese Stencils" (1980), "Boxes," and "Coptic Textiles" (1981), the latter prepared by Conservator Wendy Shah, who had joined the staff part-time. In 1985 Assistant Curator Jane Ingle Ohly's beautiful show, "Cloth of Kings," demonstrated the strength of the RISD collection in just one textile technique: velvet. In 1981 "Jacquard," an important exhibition of contemporary works created on RISD's working jacquard loom, was organized by Assistant Professor of Textiles Alice Marcoux, which resulted in a number of contemporary jacquard fabrics being added to the collection (see Cynthia Schira's "Night Games," cat. no. 112). This exhibition traveled nationwide, as did the famous exhibition of contemporary weavings, "Textiles for the Eighties," organized by Assistant Professor Maria Tulokas, Head of the Textile Department of the School, in 1985.

"Costumes in Context," 1979

A renewed effort to support the Costume and Textiles Department, which had finally been officially created in 1977,[21] came in 1985 when, after the retirement of Miss Fayerweather, Director Frank Robinson combined several part-time posts in the Department into a long-needed full-time curatorship, to augment the overworked assistant curator. In 1985, he was able to appoint Susan Anderson Hay curator, and in 1987, Pamela A. Parmal joined the staff as the new assistant curator. In 1986, Mrs. Hay produced the first large exhibition of costume ever held in the Museum, and the first in any museum to show a comprehensive range of American fashion design, "American Style," an exhibition which gained nationwide publicity and has led to a number of costume donations. "A Thousand Years of Textiles" in 1987 showed some of the great masterpieces of the textile collection, including many objects published in this handbook. An exhibition, "Batik: Northern Javanese Textiles from the Collection of Inger McCabe Elliott," in 1987, was the occasion for a scholarly symposium on Indonesian textiles that attracted an overflow crowd.

Remembering the dicta of the founders of RISD that the School and Museum are branches of the same undertaking, the staff of the Department continues to hold classes for students. A new program involves the teaching in the Museum of a required course in Costume History taught by the Apparel Design staff, which takes place each fall with examples from the collection discussed by the curators. Other subjects dealt with by the curators have been printed textiles, embroidery, compound weaves, Bauhaus weavings, 1920s and 1930s evening costume, and costume by designers Claire McCardell and Bonnie Cashin, all of which can be excellently illustrated from the collection.

Eleanor Fayerweather shows Assistant Curator Mary Louise Fazzano one of the Museum's ballgowns by Charles James, 1980 or 1981

Thanks to the steady support of the Fine Arts Committee of the Museum, important purchases, the first since the 1940s, have again begun to be made, such as the splendid Nasca mantle (cat. no. 87), the 18th century dress of

21. Memo, Stephen Ostrow to "Staff," n.d.,
    RISD Museum Archives.

The installation of "Textiles for the Eighties"
transformed the Waterman galleries, 1985

"A Thousand Years of Textiles," 1987

printed cotton by William Kilburn (cat. no. 69), and the Elizabethan embroidered cap (cat. no. 52). In 1985 the Museum Associates honored retiring Curator Eleanor Fayerweather with the purchase of two fine examples of 18th century French dress, a subject in which she was especially interested (cat. nos. 61 and 62). Many generous donors have added to these pieces; in the last decade their gifts have included a splendid collection of Fortuny cotton fabrics, several fine quilts, 16th to 18th century European silks, and contemporary Japanese clothing, among many others.

In the end, this brief history of the RISD collection can be seen as an essential and continuous collaboration between devoted donors like these and the founders, directors, and curators of the Museum, each contributing their own particular expertise and enthusiasms to the collection of costume and textiles. Thanks to them the collection today is a strong general one, illustrating the history of weaving, surface decoration, and dress. Thanks to Eliza Radeke, who set the direction, it is rich in Asian and ethnographic textiles; to L. Earle Rowe it owes not only its fine Coptic and Peruvian textiles, but its European tapestries; the Asian textiles given by Lucy Truman Aldrich are some of the best in this country, and the collection of Noh robes has been called the finest in the United States. Twentieth century textiles are especially strong because the directors and curators of the 1940s and 1950s saw that RISD could make a unique contribution in this area.

With a few exceptions, the Museum today lives up to the hopes of its founders, who looked forward to a collection "of all the kinds of beautiful fabrics that have been made: in order to teach the students to make beautiful fabrics in their turn."[22] This handbook is evidence of that, and of the commitment and discernment of all who have played a part in its development over the years.

SUSAN ANDERSON HAY

22. Appeal for contributions, 1913, RISD
    Archives.

Zairean, *Ceremonial Skirt*, early 20th century (cat. no. 6)

Persian, *Tomb Cover*, early 18th century, detail (cat. no. 19)

Indian, *Reynolds Coverlet,* ca. 1640–1650 (cat. no. 22)

Chinese, *Ch'i-fu*, ca. 1873 (cat. no. 38)

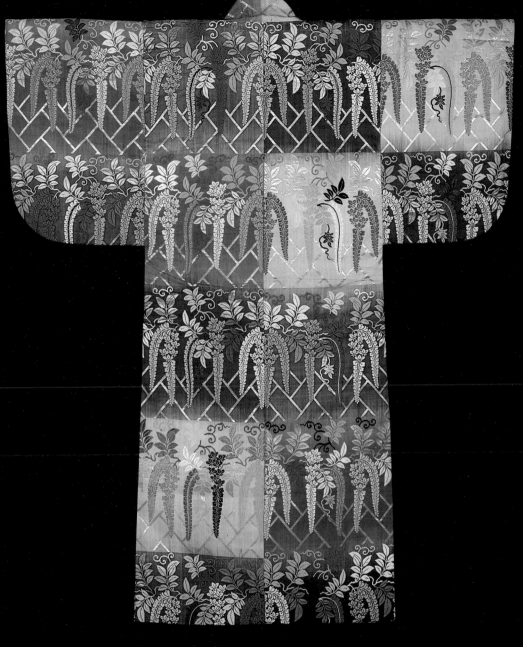

Japanese, *Noh Robe*, 1750–1800 (cat. no. 41)

English, *Man's Nightcap*, ca. 1580 (cat. no. 52)

French or Italian, *Chasuble*, mid-18th century (cat. no. 64)

French, *Court Train*, early 19th century (cat. no. 72)

French, *Unmade Dress Length*, ca. 1862, detail (cat. no. 75)

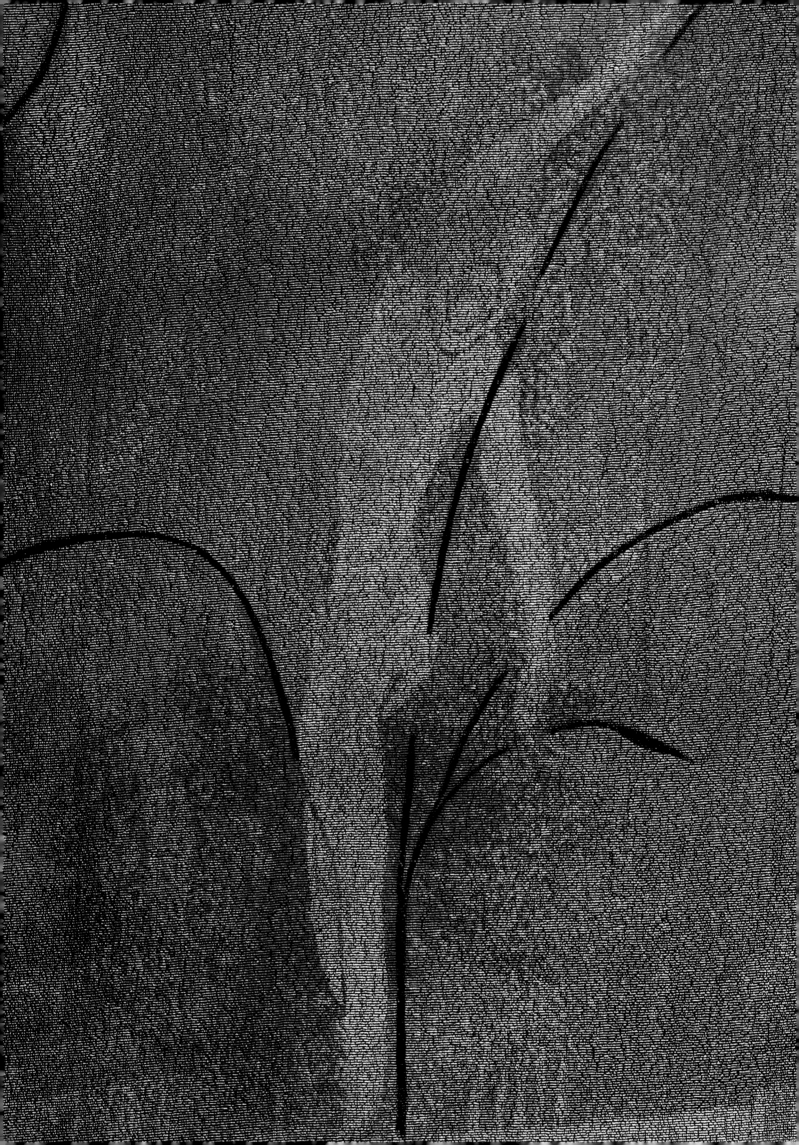

Italian, *Lace Collar and Cuffs*, early 20th century (cat. no. 84)

Paul Poiret, *Evening Coat*, ca. 1925, detail (cat. no. 82)

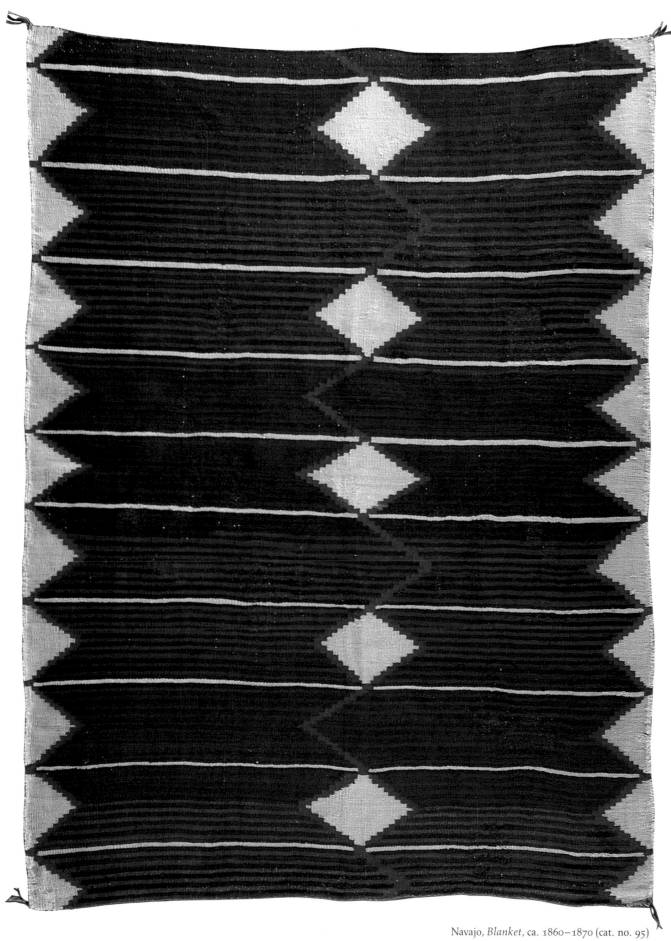

Navajo, *Blanket*, ca. 1860–1870 (cat. no. 95)

Peruvian, *Mantle*, 300–200 B.C., detail (cat. no. 86)

Nabby Martin, *Sampler*, 1786 (cat. no. 103)

Charles James, *Balloon Dress*, 1955 (cat. no. 109)

The Catalogue

The entries begin in Africa and go eastward to Polynesia, China and Japan, then treat Europe and South and North America. In general, entries within regions are chronological; American ethnographic materials, arranged by country and chronologically within each country, are followed by Colonial and later American works. European textiles, because of their shared history, are treated as a unit. All dimensions are in inches, unless otherwise noted; height is followed by width, and where appropriate, by depth. Fitted costume that is cut-and-sewn to size is measured lengthwise at center back, unless otherwise indicated. Footnote references refer by short title to works listed in the Selected Bibliography, pp. 157–159; isolated references have full bibliographic citations. Frequently used abbreviations are as follows:

Bulletin. Bulletin of the Rhode Island School of Design, 1913–1979.

Handbook. Carla Mathes Woodward and Franklin W. Robinson, eds., *A Handbook of the Museum of Art, Rhode Island School of Design*, rev. ed. Providence, Rhode Island: Museum of Art, Rhode Island School of Design, 1988.

Lucy T. Aldrich Collection. Lucy T. Aldrich Collection of Japanese Nō Drama Costumes and Priest Robes. Providence, Rhode Island: Art Museum, Rhode Island School of Design, 1937.

Museum Notes. Museum Notes, Rhode Island School of Design, 1943 to date.

1900 to Now. 1900 to Now: Modern Art from Rhode Island Collections. Providence, Rhode Island: Museum of Art, Rhode Island School of Design, 1988.

Cynthia Schira, *Night Games*, 1981, detail (cat. no. 112)

Moroccan, High Atlas region, ca. 1910

HANBEL
Wool; plain weave and twill with
supplementary wefts. 117″ x 53¼″

Gift of Miss Julia Brewster in memory of
Mrs. Elizabeth Newton Bosworth. 43.260

The hanbel or hamel is a familiar textile
type in North Africa, where it is woven
and used by Berber tribeswomen in
Morocco, Libya, and Algeria. Woven on a
vertical loom for domestic use, the hanbel
may be used, according to where it is
made, as a blanket or a rug. Likewise,
although all Berber textiles woven on the
vertical loom are related in their patterning of horizontal stripes, each hanbel type
can be associated with a particular region.
In Morocco, women of the nomadic
Zemmour tribe of the Middle Atlas region
weave colorful hanbel with large exuberant
patterns which may include knots and
decorative tufts of wool. In the High Atlas
region, where the Berber tribes lead the
settled life of farmers, the hanbel is more
sober, flat woven in bands of natural colors
as in this example.

"Sober" should not, however, be taken
to mean "simple," since this hanbel is a
rich mixture of weaving techniques differing from band to band. The small motifs
at the end of each plain band are brocaded
with supplementary wefts of colored wool
and the patterned stripes vary from simple
to complex twill weaves. The central stripe
has supplementary weft patterning in a
triangular motif common in Berber textile
design and fixes the central axis of the textile without overwhelming the whole. Bert
Flint has made an interesting comparison
between these flat-woven textiles and pre-
Islamic Arab poetry, in which each line is
an entity in itself and the poem is "an
evenly sustained succession of equal parts"
and it may indeed be that the decoration of
these very traditional blankets proceeds
from a similar aesthetic.[1] The hanbel is
fringed at the upper end only, the lower
end being finished with twining.
S.A.H.

1. Bert Flint, "The Rugs of Settled and
   Nomadic Peoples: A Contrast in Expression," in Fiske, Pickering, and Yohe, *From
   the Far West: Carpets and Textiles of
   Morocco*, p. 58.

2

Bamana Tribe
Mali

BLANKET, 20th century
Cotton; strip-woven. 94″ x 50″

Gift of Barbara Deering Danielson.
82.308.41

The Dogon and other Mande-speaking tribes of West Africa see in their checkerboard patterned cloths a symbol of the ordering of the "things of this world," like the layout of fields or the sunlight on village houses.[1] This grid pattern is basic to the sculpture, architecture, and painted decorations of West Africa, and crosses both tribal and colonially established boundaries. Several peoples in Mali weave checkerboard cloths, including the Peul/Fulani, the Dogon, the Bamana, and perhaps smaller groups of the region. This makes an individual checkerboard cloth difficult to localize, at least until further fieldwork has been done. Because the Bamana produce so many checkerboard blankets as tradecloth, this one has been attributed to that area.[2]

Checkerboard blankets, or "kosso walani," are woven by men, who in West Africa produce all strip-woven cloth. Women, who weave their own cloths on wide looms, prepare the cotton yarn, cleaning and spinning it. The yarn for part of the blanket is dyed indigo, and the strips are woven with alternating blue and white rectangles, calculated to result in a checkerboard pattern when the strips are sewn together.

This blanket has a few patterned squares woven into the strips as random accents, establishing a refreshing irregularity and avoiding boredom with the repetitious grid pattern. An additional enlivening feature is the differing surface treatment of each side of the blanket, one side being brushed and softened, the other still retaining debris from incomplete cleaning of the cotton before spinning.
S.A.H.

1. De Mott, "The Spiral and the Checkerboard," pp. 17–19.
2. Monni Adams, letter to the author, October 24, 1987.

3

Ashanti Tribe
Ghanaian, Bonwire

KENTE CLOTH, early 20th century
Silk; strip woven, plain weave alternating
with basket weave, continuous and discontinuous supplementary wefts. 118″ x 92″

Walter H. Kimball Fund. 81.096

Publication: *Museum Notes*, 1982,
pp. 9–10.

detail

Perhaps the most widely known of all West African textiles is the brightly colored kente cloth. Kente cloths are woven primarily in Bonwire, a village in the Ashanti region of southern Ghana. Worn like a toga, the kente cloth is traditional male dress for the Ashanti tribe. Under the influence of the late President of Ghana, Kwame Nkrumah, kente became more than purely Ghanaian and almost the uniform of pan-Africanism.[1]

The term "kente" may have originated from the Fanti word "kenten," meaning basket, because of its basket-like design. The people of Bonwire call the cloth kente only when talking to outsiders, however, and among themselves, refer to the cloth as "Nvoduaso," "Nwentana," or "N'toma."[2] Each individual cloth also has a name, as do frequently used designs.

Strips for kente cloth are woven on a narrow handloom by men, but the important job of sewing the strips together is saved for older, respected weavers.

At one time, the wearing of kente cloths was restricted to men of high social status, but today, it is a symbol of national pride, and anyone with the means can purchase one. Wearing a locally woven kente cloth to an Islamic festival or a state affair is a celebration of tradition.

RISD's silk kente cloth is an example of the now fairly common "sika Futoro" or "gold dust" pattern, symbolic of warmth, prosperity, and long life. It illustrates the regular spacing of inlay block, "susudua." Susudua is the name of a measuring stick used by the weaver to ensure that each block is the proper length to match the total pattern of the cloth.[3]

The cloth is woven entirely of silk. At one time, silk cloth was available only by royal order, but now can be purchased fairly readily. Originally, the Ashanti acquired silk thread for weaving by unraveling imported silk cloth. Today, however, imported silk thread is available to the weavers.

Kente cloths are named very thoroughly. First, there are different names for cloths of different levels of fineness. This particular cloth falls somewhere in between "Topreko" and "Faprems," which are the second and third finest types of Ashanti cloth. Each cloth has an individual name, as does each weft design. This cloth has a five-design "head" which features such traditional patterns as "Nleyemfere," "Mpuaa Nkron," and "Nnwotoa" or "snail's bottom."[4]

R. P.

1. Lamb, *West African Weaving*, p. 22.
2. Ibid., p. 128.
3. Ibid., p. 134.
4. Smith, "Kente Cloth Motifs," pp. 36–38.

4

Hausa Tribe
Nigerian

AGBADE, early 20th century
Cotton; strip woven. 53″ x 92″

Gift of Roberta Alford Capers in memory
of John Alford. 1986.084.1

Publication: *Museum Notes*, 1987, p. 16.

This man's riding mantle, or agbade, was
made by the Islamic Hausa tribe in Northern Nigeria. Woven, sewn, and embroidered entirely by men, it may have required
six months to complete and was the product
of a collaboration involving several people.
First, the fabric, less than one inch wide,
that is seamed together to form the body
of this textile was produced by a professional weaver on a simple, narrow loom
employing a dragstone instead of a warp
beam. In this typical West African system,
the warp ends stretch out on the ground
for many yards in front of the weaver,
attached to a sledge and weighted with the
dragstone. As the weaver needs more warp
for the simple plain weave of machine-
spun cotton, he pulls on the weighted
threads, dragging the sledge closer to the
loom and providing more warp. The
finished part of the strip is then rolled onto
a beam attached to the loom. The embroidery on this mantle, designed by a specialist
who may have been a Koranic scholar, is an
elaboration of a traditional African pattern
called "aska takwas," or "eight knives,"
after the knife-like forms at the shoulder
and on the pocket. Interlaced patterns are
incorporated into the design; scholars
think that these may be derived from
Islamic design.[1]

A knotted triangular piece called the
"linzami" is purchased from a man who
specializes in making these inserts for the
front of the neck opening. It is made of the
same kind and color of thread used for the
embroidery of the gown and sewn into the
neckline. The neckline of the garment on
the wearer's right is trimmed with a
braided strip, the "sharoba," completing
the ornamentation of the agbade.

Proud horsemen, the Hausa wear their
mantles as part of their riding costume.
When worn, the sleeves of the agbade are
pleated and bunched at the shoulder, acting
as a frame for the embroidered front. Additional embroidered ornament is often
added over many years of wear, but the
excellent condition of the RISD agbade
suggests that it was not made to be worn
but rather for the export market.[2]

S.A.H.

1. Picton and Mack, *African Textiles*, pp. 99–
   101, 189–195.
2. Monni Adams, personal communication,
   1987.

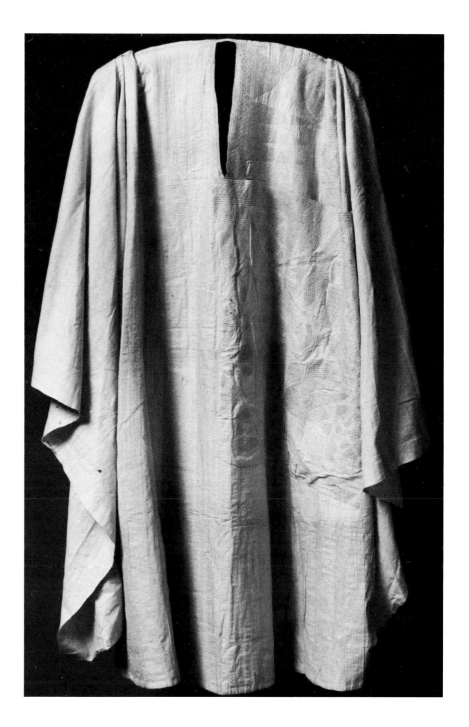

5

Sundi Tribe, Kongo People
Republic of Congo

CAP, pre-19th century
Bast fiber, possibly raffia; knotted and
looped. 10″ x 8″

Gift of Grace Abbot Fletcher. 55.128.22

Important high status articles of dress like
this cap are traditionally reserved for rulers
and chiefs among the various Kongo
people – the Kikongo, Mboma, Nyadi,
Solango, Sundi, Vili and Yombe. The cap,
a necklace of leopard teeth and coral cylin-
der beads, and bracelets and anklets of
investiture, represent the insignia of royal
authority in Kongo states.

Visible on many Kongo figure sculptures,
these prestige caps were worn by both
sexes as a royal prerogative in the complex
societies of the Kongo states. The wearing
of these caps is first recorded in Portuguese
chronicles. Early visitors to the Kongo
such as Rui de Pina (1501–1521), João de
Barros (1552) and Garcia de Resende
(1622) described ceremonial caps of Kongo
kings and nobility worn at welcoming ceremonies in Soyo and in Mbanza.

In spite of the continued erosion of the
traditional political system, in decline since
the colonial period, individuals of high
social status today still continue to wear
looped and knotted fiber caps, called "mpu"
or "pu" in the Kikongo language, as symbols of social prestige and authority. Such
individuals usually own a set of caps for
various occasions.

Attributed to the Sundi, the RISD cap is
closely related to examples in several European collections dating from the 18th
century, but an example in the Danish
National Museum was collected sometime
in the 17th century.

The RISD cap is divided into three distinct sections. The top, where the process
of hand looping and knotting pineapple or
raffia begins, shows a distinct spiral pattern. A wide band is next decorated with
complex geometric designs. The edge is
finished with a wide plain band.

Its geometric design represents only one
example of the repertoire available to the
artists of the Kongo states, and is typical
of many other central African peoples
including the Kuba tribes (compare cat. no.
6). On the artistic level the amazing integ-
ration of visual and hand skills of the African artists, who work without the help of
patterns or samples, is evident in the clar-
ity and balance of design and form seen in
this royal cap which displays great skill and
control.
T.G.

6

Kuba People, Bushong Group
Zairean, Kasai-Sankuru region

CEREMONIAL SKIRT, early 20th century
Raffia; embroidered. 26″ x 66½″

Mary B. Jackson Fund. 81.079

Publication: *Museum Notes*, 1982, p. 10;
Handbook, p. 299.

Elaborately ornamented wrap-around skirts such as this example remain an important element of traditional Kuba costume and are still worn by women dancers on ceremonial occasions, or by masked men impersonating female characters.

Woven palm fiber introduced into Zaire in the 17th century largely replaced the fragile beaten bark fabric traditionally used for clothing. Two rare examples of Kuba ceremonial skirts dating to the turn of the century (one in the Brooklyn Museum, and one in the Indiana University Art Museum, Bloomington) have central sections composed of small triangular pieces of beaten bark in patchwork technique, whose borders, embroidered with linear geometric designs, are similar in pattern to those of the RISD skirt. This reveals a close relationship between the three skirts and suggests that they were all made by the Bushong tribe around 1900.

The central panel of the Bushong ceremonial skirt is usually of a single color; natural beige and varying shades of red are most popular. The red appearance of the RISD skirt is primarily due to staining by the red earth of the region, traces of which remain encrusted in the pile. The singular design motif of the central panel of the RISD skirt is arranged in a repeat pattern. This regularity, however, is offset by the haphazard piecing of the panels without consideration for a continuous pattern.

The production of a ceremonial skirt involves an interesting alternation of work by men and women. Raffia fibers from the leaves of the palm *Raphia vinifera* are prepared by women and children, men set up and operate the single-heddle loom, and women dye and embroider the cloth. To create the velvety effect, strands of fiber are drawn through the woven cloth, then cut, and the ends brushed with the cutting blade so that short tufts are formed. The frequent repetition of this stitch produces the plush surface which has commonly been called "Kasai velvet."[1] In working out a design composition, Kuba women use neither sample patterns nor sketches on the cloth; they work directly from models in their minds.

A highly ornamented skirt such as the RISD example would take several years of part-time effort to complete and would form part of a total costume which distinguishes the social position of the wearer. Decorated cloths are also used as gifts in establishing relations of reciprocity, as compensation in legal settlements, or as burial shrouds that affirm the status of the deceased. The strong social importance of these decorated garments is probably the reason European trade cloth has been so slow to be accepted and why the art of raffia weaving and embroidery has not died out.
T.G.

1. Adams, "Kuba Embroidered Cloth,"
   pp. 24–39, 106–107.

Color plate, page 25

7

Egyptian, Old or Middle Kingdom, before
1450 B.C.

BURIAL CLOTH
Linen; plain weave. 51" x 40"

Gift of Brown University. 22.061

Most of the artifacts which remain from the
culture of Pharaonic Egypt are what archaeologists call grave-goods: items interred
with the dead. Linen textiles are a prominent feature of Egyptian entombments
either as domestic linens and clothing
stored in baskets and chests or, more commonly, as mummy wrappings.

Egypt was well known in the ancient
world for its production of linen cloth, the
earliest known piece dating to 4500 B.C. It
has been suggested that the annual Nile
floods led to the accidental discovery of the
linen fiber since the stalks of the flax plants
which grew along the river would have
rotted and dried naturally as the waters
receded.

The cultivation of flax and manufacture
of linen became an important industry in
Egypt and was illustrated in wall paintings
and in small models of weavers' shops. The
linen yarns were prepared by twining, a
process in which small bundles of fibers
were overlapped slightly and spliced by rolling them together in the S-direction,
which is linen's natural twist. Two or more
of these moist "rovings" were twined, again
in an S-direction, to form the yarn. The
natural S-twist strengthened the splicing
and the twining as the yarn dried.

Until about 1400 B.C., Egyptians used a
horizontal or ground loom, the design of
which helps to explain another distinguishing feature of Old and Middle Kingdom
Egyptian textiles: the fringe along one
selvedge. There were generally more warp
than weft yarns per inch in the cloth, but
the loom was set up without a reed or
other separating device to maintain the
spacing of the warp threads as the cloth
was woven. It is thought that the long
loops of weft enabled the weaver to
straighten out any deformation in the
width of the cloth by pulling back on the
excess. Several other types of selvedge
fringe techniques have been recorded,
including one in which extra yarns were
woven in and out of the selvedge, leaving
long loops at the edge.[1]

It is generally considered unlikely that all
of the cloth found in Egyptian tombs was
made specifically for burial. Identification
marks found on some pieces indicate that
household and personal linens were used
and that people were sometimes wrapped
in or buried with goods bearing another
owner's mark. The RISD cloth is similar in
size and quality to those used either as a
final wrapping for a mummy, or to drape
around statues or figures left in the tomb.
M.S.

1. Needler, "Three Pieces of Unpatterned Linen
From Ancient Egypt," pp. 238–251.

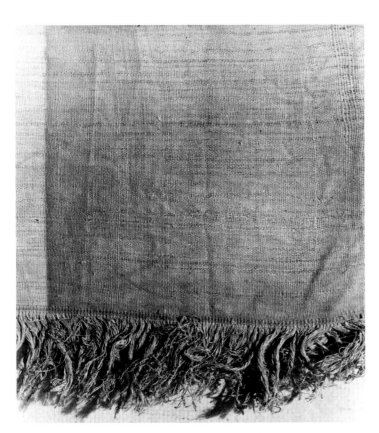

detail

8

Egyptian, Pre-Ptolemaic, before 330 B.C.

TUNIC
Linen; uncut pile. 25½″ x 22½″

Gift of Denman W. Ross. 12.071

Tunics are an ancient form of costume, dating at least to Pharaonic times, and continued to be worn in Coptic Egypt. Long thought to date to the 3rd or 4th century A.D., this tunic has recently been reassigned to a much earlier date on the basis of an analysis of its cut and weave.

Made for a child, it is constructed of a linen plain weave fabric with supplementary wefts forming the three-quarter inch pile. Although this technique continued to be used for many centuries, the fine weight of the threads and the thickness of the pile suggest an early date for the tunic.

The cut of the garment is also significant. In Coptic Egypt, tunics were woven in a cross form in one piece, then seamed together on the arms and the sides. The front and back were identical and a horizontal slit served for passage of the head. In this tunic, the main body has been woven in one piece, but the sleeves are separate pieces that have been sewn on. The narrow shape of the skirt is also typical of tunics made before the advent of Greek and Roman influence, when the loose drapery of the classical tunic and toga caused the Egyptian tunic also to become wider and looser.

The pile was intended to create warmth in the sometimes chilly Egyptian climate, and the tunic was probably worn pile side in.
S.A.H.

1. I am grateful to Anna Gonosová for much of the information in this entry.

9

Egyptian, 5th century A.D.

COVER
Linen, wool; tapestry, weft wrapping, and
eccentric wefts. 20" x 16"

Gift of Mrs. Henry D. Sharpe. 78.131

Any discussion of textiles from Egypt in
the years between the division of the
Roman Empire in the 3rd and 4th centuries
and the 7th century, when Egypt fell to the
Arabs, must face a problem of terminol-
ogy. The term "Coptic," which is often
applied to works of art dating to these centuries, most frequently implies to the modern reader that the works were produced
by Christians in Egypt. In reality the word
"Copt" is derived from ancient Greek
"Aiguptios," and refers to the inhabitants
of Egypt regardless of religion. Indeed, the
art of this period employs pagan and Christian cosmology, and refers as well to the
classical tradition which survived alongside
paganism and Christianity well into late
antiquity. This cover is an example of this
ambiguity of subject and meaning, in a
form particularly associated with the
height of Coptic art in the 5th century.

Trilling points out that most surviving
patterned textiles from late antiquity are
tapestries, ranging from small tunic decorations to large hangings. Their survival
occurred because Egyptians still buried
their dead in elaborate clothing and with
textile accouterments, although the practice of mummification had ceased by this
time, and because the enveloping sand
combined with the extremely dry climate
assisted their preservation.[1]

Technically the cover is of tapestry over
triple warps, with slit and dovetailed weft-
wrapping and eccentric wefts forming the
central section, while the long looped pile
edge is of plain weave linen with supplementary wefts and weft loops at regular
intervals.

A number of surviving covers and curtains attributed to the 4th and 5th centuries employ this technique, including
some in the Textile Museum, Washington,
D.C., with various tapestry patterns.
Baginski and Tidhar illustrate a similar
cover with exactly the same bird, reversed
and in a different border, in the Haifa
Museum.[2] Trilling suggests that tapestries
with similar styles and subject matter be
placed in groups to aid in the identification
of individual workshops, and this group of
textiles in particular forms a tantalizing
assemblage.[3]

The pattern of the tapestry in the RISD
example shows a reference to classical
realism and attention to nature in the
depiction of the bird, possibly a quail, but
the surrounding border is a geometric
abstraction probably deriving from the
earlier realistic double-vine motif that
referred to the Christian Church or the
cult of Dionysus. In this context the bird
may symbolically refer to the soul, a survival from ancient Egyptian iconography.[4]
Because of this characteristic juxtaposition
of realism and abstraction, the cover has
been dated stylistically to the 5th century,
while with its combination of motifs and
traditions, it mirrors the diversity of Coptic
Egypt.
S.A.H.

1. Trilling, *The Roman Heritage*, pp. 13, 29.
2. Baginski and Tidhar, *Textiles from Egypt*,
   p. 41.
3. Trilling, p. 18.
4. Ann Van Rosevelt, "Coptic Textiles: An
   Introduction," in Kelsey Museum of
   Archaeology, *The Art of the Ancient Weaver*,
   p. 20.

10

Egyptian, Coptic, 4th or 5th century A.D.

COVER OR HANGING
Linen, wool; tapestry weave. 30″ x 25½″

Gift of Mrs. Jesse H. Metcalf. 39.126

Covers of this size and completeness are rare in museum collections. Objects for domestic use in 4th or 5th century Egypt, still ruled by Romans from Constantinople, small covers like this would have been used on tabletops or as small wall hangings. The decoration of this cover is Hellenistic in its inspiration and has served to assign it an early date. The realistic birds in this cover relate to the bird of 78.131 (cat. no. 9) dated to the early 5th century, and other fragments with birds or similar floral ornaments in the Louvre, the Textile Museum, Washington, D.C., and the Victoria and Albert Museum have also been given dates from the 4th to the 6th centuries. The two central bands are probably derived from the pattern of laurel wreaths, and the braid interlace band is another common classically derived motif.

This naturalistic rather than geometric ornament is as typical of early Coptic textiles as it is of late Roman wall-painting, mosaics, and other decorative arts objects. Because most Coptic textiles, including this cover, do not have archaeological dates, these stylistic comparisons provide the only clues to possible dates for the textiles.

This cover, which has most of all four of its edges, must have been made on a vertical loom, a descendant of the ancient Egyptian loom depicted in tomb paintings as long ago as 2000 B.C.[1] This loom had two uprights, and, lashed to the uprights, two beams to mark the top and the bottom. The loom was warped continuously, looping around both top and bottom beams, so that when weaving was finished four selvedges were present, as in this textile. The bottom of the textile retains the loops where the bottom beam was pulled out. The top has been finished by the application of a twined band.

S.A.H.

1. Ann Van Rosevelt, "Coptic Textiles: An Introduction," in Kelsey Museum of Archaeology, *The Art of the Ancient Weaver*, p. 10.

11

Egyptian, Coptic, early 5th century A.D.

ROUNDEL AND CORNER FRAGMENTS
Wool; tapestry weave. Roundel: D. 10″;
corner fragments, 17½″ x 21″

Gift of Denman W. Ross. 12.052 and
12.053

Also early arrivals in the Museum's collection, this unusually finely-woven pair of tunic decorations in an interlace pattern still bears fragments of the linen garment into which they were woven. The round fragment is a shoulder decoration, and the corner band may be a clavus or neckline decoration, or a part of a decorative band around the bottom of the tunic.

The interlace motif was a common one in textiles, particularly in tunic ornamentation, but also occurs in other decorative arts of the period. The interlace tunic ornaments were usually purple, and seem to have been restricted to the period between 300 A.D. and the mid-6th century.[1] Trilling has developed a chronology based on several dated interlace tunic medallions, which proceeds from simplicity to complexity and intricacy of design in the 5th century, and declines into unimaginative obscurity by the 6th century. According to this chronology, these fragments should belong to the early 5th century, when complicated interlaces of fine construction yet balanced, supple design, were being produced.[2]

Probably woven in a workshop that specialized in tunic weaving, these fragments are of extremely fine wool so as not to disrupt the light weight of the linen plain-weave tunic. The tapestry was woven in white and purple wool yarns, while the outlines of the interlace design were made by carrying an eccentric linen weft throughout the weaving, wrapping it around the purple tapestry and floating it across the diagonals, a technique sometimes picturesquely called "the flying shuttle."
S.A.H.

1. Trilling, *The Roman Heritage*, p. 104.
2. Ibid., p. 106.

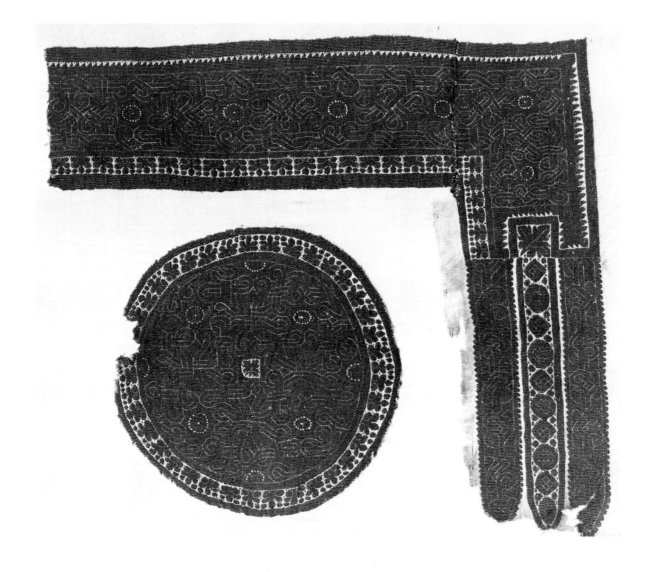

12

Egyptian, Coptic, found at Akhmim,
7th–8th century A.D.

CUSHION COVER
Linen, wool; tapestry weave. 31″ x 28″

Gift of Stephen O. Metcalf. 10.009

One of the earliest pieces to be given to the
collection, this wool and linen cover, like
most Coptic textiles, has neither provenance nor date, having come from a grave
excavated in the haphazard and sometimes
clandestine manner of the late 19th and
early 20th centuries. When compared with
39.126 (cat. no. 10), the greater density of
the weave suggests that this textile may
have been used as a cushion-cover rather
than on a table-top. In a late Roman house
centered around an open peristyle, with
walls covered with decorative murals and
floors with mosaic, little visual room
remained for furniture or textiles. But
when most of the furniture consisted of
wooden couches or benches, cushion
covers were an essential part of household
decoration, and could add to the sumptu-
ousness of a room.

This cover affords an interesting example
of the increasingly abstract ornamentation
that is deemed to be of a date later than the
classical naturalism of 39.126. The tapestry bands of this cover are much more
stylized and decorative than the motifs of
39.126, and instead of clearly recognizable
and naturalistic flowers, this cover has
abstractions of flowers, placed in small and
large geometric medallions. The stemmed
flower resembles nothing that grows, and
is contained within a static geometric border. The effect of the whole composition is
flat, and although the pattern might be
called "busy" because of the presence of so
many differing small motifs, its general
effect is static and decorative rather than
lively and naturalistic.

Like 39.126, this textile has four selvedges, indicating that it also was made on
an upright tapestry loom. Ewa Wipszycka
in 1965 discovered documents showing the
existence of a group of "cushion weavers"
in Antinoë, and it is probable that this
cushion came from such a workshop,
devoted to the weaving of pillow covers
and the construction of the cushions themselves.[1] It is finished with a band of
twining at the top.

According to a notation in the accession
book in the registrar's office of the
Museum, the piece was found at Akhmim,
although no further documentation exists.
S.A.H.

1. Wipszycka, *L'Industrie Textile dans l'Égypte
   Romaine*, pp. 119–121.

13

Egyptian, Fatimid, 12th century

FRAGMENT
Silk; plain weave, with metallic thread and silk tapestry. 5" x 9½"

Museum Works of Art Fund. 47.622

In Sasanian Persia (224–651 A.D.), textiles in the form of robes of honor were given by rulers to convey and establish favor. These robes had much value and were a symbol of the ruler's power. Often they had the ruling sovereign's inscription or symbol along the borders. These borders, worked in embroidery or woven in tapestry weave, were known as "tiraz." After the Muslim invasion of Persia the custom of the tiraz persisted and later, words giving praise to God were added; these laudatory inscriptions were thought to be a good augury for the man wearing the tiraz.

When the Muslims invaded Egypt they brought with them the tiraz. The custom was so common by this time that the word tiraz had also come to mean the workshop, usually attached to the courts, in which the fabrics were woven. During the Abbasid and Tulunid periods in Egypt (8th–10th centuries), tiraz bands were usually embroidered, but during the next dynasty, that of the Fatimids, tapestry woven bands became the more prevalent form. In the early Fatimid period inscriptions were woven in Kufic script, but as the period progressed they became more and more debased, and Kufic was eventually replaced during the 12th century with Nashki

script. The Museum's silk tiraz inscription repeats the phrase "Glory" ("al-'Izz") in Nashki.[1]

This silk fragment is very similar to a group of fragments found in the Leipzig Kunstgewerbemuseum, the Staatliche Museen of Berlin, and the Victoria and Albert Museum of London. All of the fragments show similarities in material, technique, and design. Kühnel suggested in his catalogue of early Islamic textiles from Egypt in Berlin, that because of the many similarities between these existing fragments, they were probably woven in the same workshop, one in which state garments were made, and are from the same time period.[2] The similarity is especially marked between the Museum's fragment and one in Berlin. Both textiles are shot silk with yellow warps and salmon colored wefts. The fineness of the ground contrasts sharply with the tiraz bands made of silk and metallic thread tapestry. The inscription of the fragment in Berlin is simple, like the example in the RISD Museum, repeating "Power" again and again in Nashki.

P.P.

1. Translation by Scott Redford, Sackler Museum, Harvard University.
2. Kühnel, *Islamische Stoffe aus Ägyptischen Gräbern*, pl. 23.

14

Turkish, mid-16th / mid-17th century

CUSHION COVER
Silk and cotton; satin weave, silk and metallic (now missing) supplementary weft, silk cut pile velvet. 43" x 23¼"

Gift of Mrs. Gustav Radeke. 16.003

Publication: *Handbook*, p. 275.

Süleyman the Magnificent (1494–1566), whose Sultanate marks the height of the Ottoman Empire, held strict control over most aspects of his government, including the imperial design workshops, or "nakkaşhane," where design styles were created and quickly spread throughout the repertoire of decorative arts, including textiles. In the textile industry itself, strict regulations controlled both the quality and type of textiles being produced. Regulations seem to have also extended to how specific types of textiles were to be used. Although no written records survive, among the textiles in the Topkapi Sarayi in Istanbul a hierarchy is apparent in which brocaded figured silks were used for ceremonial robes, velvets like the Museum's were used for furnishings like draperies, curtains, cushions, and pillows, and silk embroidery was reserved for clothing accessories and more intimate furnishing fabrics.[1]

The Museum's velvet was probably a bench cover and would have been used in a room along with a profusion of textiles covering walls, floors, and cushions. Termed "çatma" by the Ottomans, velvet of this type was produced in great quantities. Voided velvet, pile, and satin weaves were combined in çatma with gold or silver supplemental brocading wefts. In the Museum's velvet the metallic lamella wound around a white silk core has almost totally disappeared, leaving small traces only where the brocading borders the pile weave sections.

The design of the cover, a compartmentalized fan-shaped carnation enclosing carnation and tulip buds, was one of the most popular motifs in Ottoman Turkey. Textiles incorporating small naturalistic buds with overall geometric patterning were first created in the "nakkaşhane" by the designer Kara Memi (fl. 1540s–1560s). One of the earliest existing examples, a kaftan in the Topkapi Palace in Istanbul has an overall geometric pattern with small tulips and carnation blossoms incorporated into the design, but since the style continued through the mid-17th century, specific dating of the Museum's velvet has not been possible.
P.P.

1. Walter Denny, "Textiles," in Petsopoulos, *Tulips, Arabesques, and Turbans*, p. 132.

15

Turkish, Bursa, late 16th/early 17th
century

DALMATIC
Silk; lampas, 4/1 satin foundation weave,
3/1 twill supplemental weave, discontinuous supplementary metallic patterning
wefts. 52″ x 51″

Museum Appropriation. 28.008

Publications: Riefstahl, "Greek Orthodox
Vestments and Ecclesiastical Fabrics," pp.
359–373; *Handbook*, p. 274.

Like that of the Roman Catholic Church,
the history of Greek Orthodox vestments
is full of elaborate and costly examples.
The shapes and styles of Eastern vestments
differed slightly from those of the Western
church, but the textiles and embroidered
decorations were just as luxurious. This
tradition persisted even after the conquest
of Constantinople, the capital of the
Byzantine empire and center of the
Orthodox faith, in 1453 by the Turks. The
Greek Orthodox community living under
Byzantine rule, primarily composed of
Greeks, Serbians, Bulgarians, and Ruma-
nians, was allowed to continue practicing
its religion under Ottoman rule. The
Museum's dalmatic, made of silk woven in
the Ottoman city of Bursa, shows both
Greek and Turkish influence and is a
graphic illustration of the polyglot nature
of the Ottoman Empire.

Bursa was conquered by the Turks in
1326 and became the first capital of the
Ottoman Empire. Its importance rested
in the fact that it was on the silk route
between Asia and the West, making it one of
the most important entrepôts in the silk
trade between Asia and Europe, and by
1468 it dominated the silk route, acting as
a center for the reexportation or processing
of raw silk from Persia and the Far East to
Europe. But Bursa also became an important weaving center within the Ottoman
Empire, supplying the demands of the
court and providing export goods. Because
of Bursa's role in the international silk
trade the industry was open to a variety of
outside influences and demands from
those countries and clients for which it was
providing the silks. This combination of
design inspirations became one of the
characteristics of Bursa silks, and in the
silk designs one can find influences from
China, Byzantium, Persia, Italy, and
Greece.

The Museum's dalmatic shows the influence of a variety of sources. It is an unusual
example of a figural silk woven in Turkey,
where ordinarily, Islamic law forbade the
representation of figures. But for this vest-
ment, intended for the Greek Orthodox
market, the designer of the textile took his
inspiration from Greek textiles woven for
the use of the Orthodox church.[1] Jesus
Christ is enthroned as in the Byzantine
tradition of the Pantokrator. He is surrounded by the symbols of the four
evangelists; the eagle of St. John, the
angel of St. Matthew, the ox of St. Luke,
and the lion of St. Mark. The figure of
Christ is also flanked by the Greek inscription *IC XC* and *NIKA* or *IESOUS CHRISTOS
NIKA*, "Jesus Christ conquers." In typical
Turkish fashion the designer could not
leave out the ubiquitous flowers so prominent in Ottoman textiles, the carnation
and the rosebud.

The weaving technique of the silk cor-
responds to similar silks woven in Bursa,
with little or no gold thread used, and is
typical of silks woven during the late 16th
and early 17th centuries.
P.P.

1. Riefstahl, "Greek Orthodox Vestments and
   Ecclesiastical Fabrics," fig. 1.

16

Turkish, late 16th century

CURTAIN
Linen, silk; darned embroidery.
85" x 57¼"

Bequest of Lucy Truman Aldrich. 55.563

The Ottoman Turkish empire was formed from a variety of nomadic tribes originally from Central Asia where a long tradition existed of colorfully embroidered portable furnishings which could be easily packed away. These included wall hangings, floor coverings, and cushions, which continued to be made in the reign of the Ottoman sultans.

The earliest surviving Ottoman embroideries date from the 16th century, when embroideries for the court were supplied by court workshops, and those for domestic use were either completed in the home or bought from workshops not attached to the courts. The Museum's curtain was probably made in one of these workshops during the second half of the 16th century, making it one of the rare domestic embroideries to survive from this time.

The pieces made in domestic workshops were often inspired by fashionable woven textiles, which were extremely expensive, and served as cheaper substitutes for them. The design of this curtain is based on Ottoman textiles of the second half of the 16th century, when ogival patterns borrowed from Egyptian Mamluk textiles, Chinese or Chinese-inspired Iranian silks, or European silks became part of the design repertoire.[1] The design of this curtain closely resembles the design of the woven silk in a royal kaftan from the mid-16th century now in the Topkapi Palace in Istanbul, whose pattern of large pine cones set in a half drop repeat, creating a negative ogival lattice, was fashionable.[2] The design of the Museum's curtain is extremely simplified and stylized, further suggesting a workshop origin.

Most embroideries were made on fine loosely-woven linen plain weave grounds using a darning stitch in which the ground threads must be counted before being covered over with silk stitching. In the case of the Museum's curtain, the darning pattern is a 3/1 twill in which the thread is passed over three threads of the plain weave ground and under one.
P.P.

1. Walter Denny, "Textiles," in Petsopoulos, *Tulips, Arabesques and Turbans*, p. 128.
2. Atil, *The Age of Sultan Süleyman the Magnificent*, p. 192.

17

Persian, Seljuk, 12th century

FRAGMENT
Silk; plain weave with supplementary
wefts and inner warps. 9" x 24½"

Museum Appropriation. 36.010.

Publications: *Bulletin*, 1937, pp. 74–77;
Handbook, p. 160.

During the reign of the Seljuk Turks a
thriving economy grew up in which excess
wealth created a demand for luxury goods.
One of the most important of those goods
was silk, woven both for export and for
domestic consumption, primarily as burial
cloths.

The use of silk in burial for both shrouds
and pall covers was a common practice.[1]
The Seljuks were Sunni Muslims, adher-
ing to the tenets of the Koran where "it is
said that the raiment of the people of
paradise will be silk." In the ascetic tenden-
cies of early Islam this often expressed
itself in the form that he who wears silk in
this world, shall not wear it in the next.[2]
Thus the Seljuks disdained the wearing of
silk, preferring that of wool and linen, but
because of courtly traditions as well as the
dictates of the Koran, silk had an important
place in Islamic burial customs. The silk
textiles themselves bear witness to this
association with death. The inscription on
the Museum's fragment is translated "Be
not secure from death in any place nor at
any breath."[3]

Many of the silks which survive from
medieval Persia were excavated from burial
sites in the city of Rayy, located just outside Isfahan. Rayy was a capital of Seljuk
Iran, and tomb towers near Rayy provided
a large number of textile finds through
uncontrolled excavation in the early 20th
century. However, because of technical and
stylistic similarities they can be traced back
to the necropolis of Rayy.

The RISD piece shares many similarities
with known textiles attributed to Rayy. It
is woven in plain weave with supplementary wefts and inner warps, a common
type of Islamic weave, in use since the time
of the Sasanians, who ruled Iran until the
Islamic conquest in the mid-7th century.
The arts of the Sasanians were extremely
well developed and traditional Iranian
features persisted into the reign of the
Seljuks. The medallion enclosing heraldic
animals, shown on the Museum's fragment,
was a common device of the Sasanians and
can be seen on the clothing of the figures
depicted in the rock carvings at the Sasanian
site of Taq-i Būstan. The medallion, surrounded by an inscription in Kufic and
elaborate foliage derived from the tree of
life, is common in Seljuk textiles of the
12th century.
P.P.

1. Shepherd, "Medieval Persian Silks in Fact
   and Fancy," p. 23.
2. "Harir" in *Encyclopaedia of Islam, New Edi-
   tion*, 3, London and Leiden, 1971, p. 209.
3. *Woven Treasures of Persian Art*, p. 31.

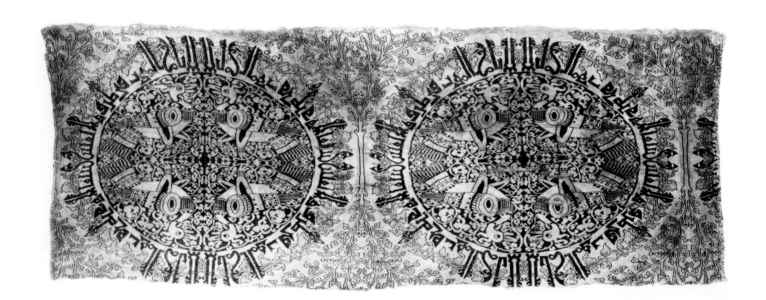

18

Persian, Safavid, second half of the 16th
century

FRAGMENT
Silk; lampas, 3/1 satin foundation weave,
2/1 twill supplemental weave. 12½" x 28½"

Museum Appropriation. 36.011

Publications: *Bulletin*, 1937, pp. 74–77;
Handbook, pp. 162–163.

With the coming to power of the Safavids
in 1499, the Mongol conquerors who had
reigned in Persia for two centuries were
ousted and a native dynasty once again
ruled Iran. The Safavids brought back a
highly developed culture and the arts,
including weaving, flourished under their
reign. The Safavids, especially the nobility,
admitted to their design vocabulary a full
range of figural representations, including
persons such as the horseman on this silk.

Subjects for the designs of Safavid textiles originated with book illustrations,
especially those from Tabriz, the first
Safavid capital, where book artists worked
closely with the state looms also situated
there. No source has yet been identified
for the Museum's textile, which depicts a
seated horseman meeting a friend. However, the style of the design can be traced
back to court painting done under the
reign of Shah Tahmasp (1524–1576),
when painters synthesized eastern and
western Iranian styles into one which
typified the luxury and elegance of the
Safavid court. This style spread to a
number of weaving centers and was in use
until the end of the 16th century.[1]

Safavid weavers are best known
for their velvet and lampas weaves. Lampas, a particular combination of two
weaves each having its own set of warps
and wefts, was in use as early as the 13th
century and by the time of the Safavids
was widely used in both the East and the
West.[2] In most Safavid textiles the foundation weave is 4/1 satin with a supple-

mental weave of 3/1 twill. The Museum's
fragment varies from this norm, having a
3/1 satin foundation weave and a 2/1 twill
supplemental weave. The possibility that
this fragment was woven outside the court,
possibly in Kashan, has been suggested by
Phyllis Ackerman in *A Survey of Persian
Art*, mainly on a stylistic basis.[3] The variation in weave structure from the norm in
this fragment lends credence to Ackerman's
hypothesis, but too little is known of
Safavid weave structures to be certain on
these grounds alone.

P.P.

1. *Handbook*, p. 163.
2. Milton Sonday, "Pattern and Weaves:
   Safavid Lampas and Velvet," in Bier, *Woven
   from the Soul, Spun from the Heart*, p. 72.
3. Ackerman, "Textiles of the Islamic Periods,"
   pp. 2091–2.

19

Persian, Safavid, early 18th century

TOMB COVER
Silk; plain weave with supplementary
wefts and triple inner warps. 132" x 29"

Bequest of Lucy Truman Aldrich. 55.536

Textiles played an important role in Islamic
life and in death. People surrounded themselves with textiles in the home, those who
could afford it dressed in beautiful silks,
and textiles often served as a sign of status
in the form of robes of honor. The dead
were dressed in silk and buried, often with
lengths of silk fabric as tomb covers and
palls.

This beautiful example of a late Safavid
tomb cover is covered with three different
inscriptions in bands which alternate
throughout the cloth in variations of

green, gold, red, and black. The inscriptions make references to Shi'a Islam, the
sect dominant during the reign of the
Safavids. The first inscription, "O Remem-
brance of the Lion of Repeated Attack! O
Husayn!"[1] makes reference to Husayn, the
grandson of Muhammad, who was mar-
tyred at the battle of Kerbala. The second
inscription makes reference to God,
Muhammad, and his son 'Ali, the father of
Husayn: "O God! O Muhammad! O 'Ali!"
The third inscription, which continues the
martial reference of the first, "Lo! We have
given thee a signal victory," is the opening
line of the Victory Sura (Surat al-Fath) of
the Koran. The three inscriptions may
mean that this tomb cover was used for a
man of high status killed in battle.

In design and calligraphic style the tomb
cover is very similar to a silk hanging published by Mehmet Aga-Oglu, in *Safawid
Rugs and Textiles*.[2] In the border of the
hanging are a series of cartouches with half

rosettes at the corners, similar to those in
the RISD piece, enclosing the inscription,
again a martial reference. This hanging is
dated 1716/1717 A.D., giving an approxi-
mate date for the Museum's tomb cover.
P.P.

1. Inscriptions translated by Scott Redford,
   Sackler Museum, Harvard University.
2. Aga-Oglu, *Safawid Rugs and Textiles*, pl. 19.

Color plate, page 26

detail

20

Indian, Gujarat, 15th century

PRINTED TEXTILE WITH HAMSA
Cotton; plain weave. 4¾" x 10¾"

Museum Appropriation. 34.759

In the late 19th century, during a search for ancient remains in the medieval Arab city of Al Fostat, a few miles south of Cairo, archaeologists discovered thousands of madder- and indigo-dyed textiles in the upper layers of the excavation. Because they were believed to be worthless "late" materials, no levels or dates were recorded and the textiles came with Egyptian provenance but no further information into museum and private collections. In 1938, the French collector R. Pfister, taking into account the similarity of their designs to Indian art, the presence of records indicating a flourishing trade between Gujarat, in India, and Moslem Egypt, and the fact that both cotton and madder dyeing were Indian monopolies in the Middle Ages, convincingly argued that the fragments found at Al Fostat were in fact Indian.[1] Recently, the textiles have been dated to between 1200 and the 18th century, making

the earliest fragments the earliest known Indian printed textiles, and among the earliest printed textiles known.[2]

The Museum owns a number of fragments whose exact provenance cannot be traced. Some of the pieces, however, are identical with published pieces from Al Fostat, and others are so similar that their identification as Al Fostat fragments is virtually certain.

The RISD pieces do not include any of the earliest dated patterns. The earliest RISD fragment appears to be 34.759, a design with geese that is identical to fragments in the Textile Museum, Washington, D.C., and in the collection of R. Pfister which have been dated to the 15th century.[3] A small fragment with abrasions and fraying edges, it is printed in brown and red brown on loosely woven cotton. The pattern has red-brown sacred geese or "hamsa" cavorting around a lotus-flower rosette, the rosettes in turn encircling a cross made of four stylized flower forms. Dark brown details highlight both geese and the tiny border fragment.

Like many of the other Al Fostat fragments of this date, the hamsa fragment is patterned with a resist, then madder dyed. In the process of madder dyeing, differing colors are created from the same dye by combining the dye with prescribed chemi-

cals called mordants, one for each color. Here, two different mordants have been brushed onto the cloth inside wax-resist patterns that were created with a wooden block. When the cloth was then dipped in a bath of madder, red-brown and brown colors emerged, depending on which mordant lay in each area.

S.A.H.

1. Pfister, *Les Toiles Imprimées de Fostat et de l'Hindoustan*, p. 29.
2. Gittinger, *Master Dyers to the World*, pp. 31–57.
3. Pfister, pp. 29ff.; Gittinger, pl. 38.

21

Indian, Golconda, ca. 1645

TENT HANGING (qanat)
Cotton; hand-painted, madder-dyed.
80¾" x 115"

Gift of Lucy Truman Aldrich. 37.010

Provenance: Amber Palace *toshkhana*,
Rajasthan

Publications: V. Murphy, "Textiles," in
*The Indian Heritage, Court Life and Arts
Under Mughal Rule*, p. 84, no 211; *Hand-
book*, p. 157; Smart, "A Preliminary
Report on a Group of Important Mughal
Textiles," pp. 7–9, fig. 5.

Indian luxury textiles, admired and
coveted in the ancient world, scaled ever
greater heights under Muslim rule. A particularly rich and inventive tradition was
centered in the Deccani sultanate of Golconda during the 17th and 18th centuries,
where a spectacular production both for
domestic and foreign markets added to the
already fabled wealth of this diamond-rich
kingdom. The exuberance of line and soft
saturated color that mark this important
tent hanging are characteristic of the best
Golconda work. Here, three niches with
alternate grounds of red, white, and purple

enclose fantastic flowering trees and plants
with roughly symmetrical arrangements
of branches and blossoms. This architectural framework encloses intensely vibrant
blossoms and palmettes in bleeding, poly-
chromed patterns on a surface thick with
wispy tendrils and darting Chinese cloud
forms. The spandrels and borders separating the niches are thickly patterned with
scrolling leaf and flower motifs in several
colors on a yellow ground. Borders at top
and bottom are filled with boldly repeating
geometric devices containing floral arabesques reminiscent of the well-known
"rumal" (cloth used as a towel, handkerchief or covering) from this area, and above
the upper border is a band of identical
flowering plants, politely ordered in rela-
tion to the turbulence below.

Ellen Smart has identified nine other
qanat panels with the same design, in the
Textile Museum, the Cooper-Hewitt
Museum, the Los Angeles County
Museum, and the National Museum of
India. These panels were originally joined,
and formed a set with a summer carpet in
the Cincinnati Art Museum. On the basis
of inventory marks in Urdu and Persian on
the back of the Cincinnati floorspread, the
spread and qanat can both be traced to the
collection of the Mughal general and raja,
Mirza Raja Jai Singh, who ruled from the
Palace of Amber in Jaipur from 1621 to

1667. It was first inventoried in 1645 in the
Amber Palace collection, proving it to be
much earlier than 1700, when it was formerly thought to have been made.[1]

Entirely hand-painted, this tent hanging
is an example of the finest of 17th century
chintzes. It was made by first drawing and
painting in the red, black, and purple areas
using mordants. The hanging was then
dyed in madder, and blue and yellow dyes
were painted onto the resulting pattern.
When the qanat fragments were still
joined, the hanging formed part of a mov-
able wall used in tents in the sultan's
encampments whenever he traveled.

The intoxicating complexity and beauty
of examples like this demonstrate the capa-
bility of large expanses of decorated cloth
to generate a sense of splendor and luxury,
and it was undoubtedly this power to alter
and transform a setting that explains much
of India's long fascination with textiles.[2]
T. L. and S. A. H.

1. Smart, pp. 5–9.
2. The first and last paragraphs of this entry
   were written by Thomas Lentz, *Handbook*,
   p. 157.

22

Indian, Golconda, ca. 1640–1650

REYNOLDS COVERLET
Cotton; hand-painted, madder-dyed.
106″ x 89″

Gift of the Glocester Heritage Society.
83.023

Provenance: Chester Reynolds, Jr.;
Glocester Heritage Society, Glocester,
Rhode Island

Publications: *Museum Notes*, 1983, p. 13;
Handbook, p. 155.

This remarkable gift to the Museum has
brought to light a unique and important
addition to a select group of 17th century
Indian painted textiles. Probably used as a
floor covering, the design format is identical to that of a pile carpet, with an outer
border of geometric and floral motifs
enclosing a central field, both of which are
hand-painted in mordants, a complicated
and time-consuming dye process that fixes
various colors to cotton fiber.

The importance of this textile clearly
lies with the contents of the central field,
where myth and imagination collide with
the physical world. Packed almost to the
point of solidity are real and imagined
flora and fauna in multiple shades of red,
brown, blue and green on a neutral
ground. Approximately 425 birds and over

400 animals from the Indian, Iranian, and
Chinese worlds swarm through a thick
mass of foliage and rock forms. Imbued
with a bright, wide-eyed tension that glori-
ously transforms the entire setting, these
creatures are the sole inhabitants of this
fantastic landscape.

Conspicuous by his absence is man, his
presence intimated only by the inclusion
of five architectural motifs in the lower
third of the field. From a distance the field
is not easily deciphered, and the fertile
imagination behind this design has
achieved a scope of vision and scale that
continually astounds with its majestic
sweep and startling swings of mood. Tem-
pering the exotic flux, however, are numerous passages of humorous anecdote and
wit that keep this world earthbound. For
every soaring stag and ecstatic blossom
there lurks a laughing feline or ludicrous
demon, and even animal combats are
defused by sly dragons and grinning carni-
vores.

Parallels to the RISD cotton are found in
a small but well-defined group of cottons
from Golconda which are now classified as
part of the "Early Coromandel Group."
Dated to 1640–1650, these works are distinguished by their pile carpet format and
Islamic subject matter drawn in large part
from the painting of early 17th century
Iran. While there are similarities of size,
style and technique with these examples,

the distinctive composition and subject
matter of the "Reynolds Coverlet" finds
no close analogues among them.

However, another Iranian strain, one
whose roots are traceable back to the fantastic landscapes of 15th century Turkman
artists in western Iran, provides an imme-
diate link. In terms of subject matter and
composition there are striking affinities
to the RISD cotton, and while Turkman
themes found their way into India via
Safavid and Mughal art, a more direct link
with Golconda is established by the
Turkman origins of the ruling Qutb-Shahi
dynasty itself. While more or less compos-
itionally true to its prototypes, the theme
is reworked here in the contemporary Golconda style and supplemented by native
additions and inventions.

The unique character of the "Reynolds
Coverlet" represents a new category for
early Coromandel painted cottons.
Although not overtly Islamic, its features
suggest a wider range of Iranian sources
for Golconda textile production in the 17th
century and reaffirms the extraordinary
ability of Golconda artists to imaginatively
recast disparate sources into a distinctly
Indian vision.
T. L.

Color plate, page 27

detail

detail

23

Indian, early 18th century

VALANCE
Cotton; hand-painted, madder-dyed.
14" x 65½"

Georgianna Sayles Aldrich Fund. 1988.017

Provenance: Josephine Howell

Publication: Irwin and Brett, *Origins of Chintz*, fig. 21, pp. 26, 32.

The newest addition to RISD's important collection of Indian painted and printed chintzes, this valance was made in the early 18th century for the Western market. Like RISD's Reynolds floor-spread and Amber Palace tent hanging, the valance is hand-painted and madder-dyed, with blue details pencilled on in indigo, but it differs from these textiles made for the Mughal aristocracy in its thoroughly Western design.

When the traders of the British East India Company first arrived in India, the textiles they bought were not brought back to the West but were traded in Indonesia for spices. Only a few "pintathoes" reached London before the 1680s, when the directors of the Company realized that chintzes made in India to British designs might sell better than the "sad red" ones heretofore imported, of which the Reynolds coverlet is possibly an example (cat. no. 22). When in 1662 the company began to send out Western designs for the Indian chintz-painters to copy, the resulting textiles began to create a sensation. Until then little used in Europe, cotton quickly caught on for its lightness in a world used to heavy linens, woolens, and silks. As well as being bright, colorful, and tremendously exotic, the patterns dyed on these cotton cloths appealed greatly because unlike European textiles printed with oils or pigments, the colors did not wash out. Once Western traders began to import chintzes "the greatest part upon white grounds," orders poured in, and between 1680 and the end of the century a veritable flood of chintzes were imported into Europe. When in 1700 English textile manufacturers forced a law forbidding their import on the grounds that English textile industries were being threatened, trade in chintzes diminished but did not stop, as many surviving examples, including this valance, prove.[1]

The fact that this valance is entirely hand-painted rather than being stamped or printed with blocks indicates that it was the highest quality chintz available. Originally it belonged to a set of hangings made for a bed, but which might have included window curtains and even curtains to cover the walls entirely, like the set purchased by Samuel Pepys for his wife in 1663. Although records of the British East India Company show that hundreds of sets including bed curtains and valances were ordered, few pieces in the actual form of valances survive. The design of this valance is also unusual because it is so European, at a time when European designs sent out to India to be copied often returned in a highly exotic, unrecognizable form. Its classical references and rinceau-like flowers are reminiscent of the designs of the French artist Jean Bérain (1638– 1711), some of which are known to have been used as sources on the Coromandel Coast of India in the early 18th century.

S.A.H.

1. Irwin and Brett give a detailed history of the chintz trade not only in Britain but with references to France, Portugal, and the Netherlands, pp. 3–34, 92–94; pl. 66 and 67.

24

Indian, 17th/early 18th century

PATKA (sash)
Cotton; plain weave, silk embroidery,
chain stitch. 128" x 25½"

Bequest of Lucy Truman Aldrich. 55.528

Close artistic ties to the Safavid court of
Persia probably account, in part, for the
ubiquitous nature of flowers in Mughal
art, but do not explain the unique naturalism found in Mughal designs. For this the
sources were European art forms, among
them herbals, brought to India in the 16th
and 17th century by European traders.[1]
Naturalistic flowering plants were copied
from these illustrated manuscripts and can
be found in the work of Mughal court
artists in the early 17th century.[2] Over
time the use of flowering plants spread to
a variety of decorative arts, including textiles. During the 17th century floral borders were commonly found on shawls and
patkas, depicting either a single flower or
bud or clusters of flowers, known as
"buta" or "bunch," as in the Museum's
patka. As this motif developed the flowers
became more and more stylized, eventually developing into the form which we are
familiar with as the paisley.

The patka provided the perfect location
for this type of ornamentation. Long a
traditional garment, it was worn with the
tailored Mughal coat, wrapped around
the waist and tied with the ends hanging
down the front. The patka was originally
very simple, without much ornamentation, but by the 17th century geometric
forms and scrolls began to decorate the
ends, and by the 1640s the form of the
Museum's patka came into use, with narrow side borders creating a frame at both
ends of the cloth to enclose the design area,
or the "pallava."[3]

Patka were decorated in a variety of
ways: some were woven on the loom and
self-patterned, others were printed, and
others were embroidered. The RISD patka
is embroidered in an extremely fine chain
stitch. The fineness of the embroidery
would date it to the 17th or early 18th century, before the arts of the Mughal empire
began their decline during the 18th century.

P.P.

1. Yale University Art Gallery, *The Kashmir
   Shawl*, pp. 26–27.
2. Stuart Cary Welch, *India, Art and Culture
   1300–1900*, New York, 1985, p. 225.
3. Gittinger, *Master Dyers to the World*, p. 71.

detail

25

Indian, Kashmir, ca. 1815

SHAWL (dochalla)
Wool; 1/2 twill, twill tapestry weave.
120½" x 51"

Gift of Mrs. E. M. Smith. 78.192.3

Perhaps the best known Indian textiles made for the Western market after the exquisite printed textiles of the 16th to 18th centuries were woolen shawls made in the late 18th to mid-19th centuries in the Indian province of Kashmir. Already being exported to Persia in the 17th century, long Kashmir shawls or "dochalla" had been part of Indian costume as waist wrappings and shoulder mantles from ancient times. But it was not until the mid-18th century, when the typical colorful "buta" decoration of Kashmir shawls began to be developed and embellished, that the shawls caught on in Europe. Beginning about 1790, evidence in French portraits of noble families indicates that long, delicate shawls so fine that they were reported to be able to pass through a gold finger ring had come into high fashion. A great supporter of the shawl trade was the Empress Josephine, who accumulated a large collection after her husband passed on to her one given to him during his Egyptian campaign. These developments did not go unnoticed in America, and shawls quickly became part of the costume of fashionable American women.

The RISD Museum owns a fascinating pair of documented Indian shawls from a single family descended from Aletta Remsen Strong, who married James Strong about 1820. This white wool twill shawl in a long shape came with an attached note reading "Aletta Strong." Called a "dochalla" in India, the form was used in India as a shoulder wrap and in the West became the classic shawl form of the early 19th century. Because the butas in this shawl are slightly abstract, and because the tapestry design intrudes into the plain twill weave field, the shawl can be dated to around 1815.[1]

The Museum also owns a shawl of slightly later date, with a longer, wider shape, marked "Aletta Remsen's marriage shawl, given to her by her husband James Strong at their wedding about 1820." It also is of fine white wool twill, with a border of butas in twill tapestry, and a buta in each corner of the field. That these shawls were saved and descended to the donor together with several other later shawls from the family, illustrates how popular and valued shawls were, not only as garments to wear, but as objects that recalled family history. For the student and observer, the Strong family shawls function as a valuable index of shawl design in the late 18th to mid-19th centuries.
S.A.H.

1. Ames, *The Kashmir Shawl*, pp. 49–58, has an extremely useful chapter on the dating of shawls by construction and measurements on which this analysis leans.

detail

26

Indian, Gujarat, 20th century

PATOLU
Silk; double ikat. 215" x 51"

Bequest of Lucy Truman Aldrich. 55.292

Double ikat patola from Gujarat in south-west India have been valued highly in both East and West. Regarded as a mark of status in India, the cloths when exported to Indonesia in particular, took on magical, lucky powers. They were collected and imitated both in India and in all of Southeast Asia, and are still worn particularly at weddings as a talisman of good luck.

Cloths called "patola" have been woven in Gujarat since at least the 16th century when they began to be mentioned in the accounts of European travelers who marveled at the beautiful colors and complex patterning of these silk cloths. Still woven and dyed today in the city of Patan, patola have both warps and wefts tie-dyed to create patterning before the cloths are woven, a process which requires precise measuring, wrapping, and dyeing of the threads, as well as great care in placing the yarns correctly on the loom.[1] Inevitable slight misalignment of the threads causes the characteristic "blurred" effect at the edges of the motifs. The fact that these extend in both warp and weft directions in patola shows that both warps and weft have been tie-dyed, giving the name "double ikat." Because of this complex procedure of production, patola were and are expensive. As early as 1500 Duarte Barbosa, a Portuguese traveler, commented on the great value of patola all over Southeast Asia.[2]

detail

detail

RISD owns three patola, all collected by Lucy Truman Aldrich in India in the 1920s. The patterning of this patolu (as it is spelled in the singular) is termed "panbhat," which means "leaf pattern"; it is the most popular patola pattern in India, and is not commonly exported. Despite the identification of the motifs in the main field as pipal leaves, not hearts, many wealthy brides of Patan wear this pattern as a wedding sari, although this is not its only use. The pattern itself goes back to ancient India where the motif can be seen in pottery of the Indus Valley culture. The other distinguishing motifs in the design are the repeated sequences in the borders, an elephant, flower, dancing girl, and parrot. This patolu has gold threads woven into one end, the "pallava," which when the patolu is wrapped as a sari, is the end that shows, the other end being tucked into the petticoat. Because of the gold stripe on this patolu, we can surmise that it was worn as a sari, even though it is shorter by more than a yard than most saris, which measure 6 or 7 yards of fabric. Other patola of this pattern have been used as odhanis, or wraps, by women, by Patanese bridegrooms as shoulder cloths, as coverings for ceremonial offerings, as ceremonial canopies and even as pieces in linings.[3] The fact that every patola scrap is used for something in this way, and that many patola (although not this one) are patched and mended, is further confirmation of their value both monetarily and as cherished family objects.

The patola made today by traditional family weavers in Patan still have traditional patterns, but interesting new patola designs are emerging both in Patan and in Andhra Pradesh using the double ikat technique to pattern cloths with modern motifs.
S.A.H.

1. Most of the information in this entry is taken from Bühler and Fischer, *Patola of Gujarat*, 1, pp. 6–28, 216.
2. Bühler, "Patola Influences in Southeast Asia," p. 5.
3. Bühler, Ramseyer, and Ramseyer-Gygi, *Patola und Geringsing*, figs. 18, 19, and 21; and Bühler and Fischer, 2, figs. 2 and 3.

27

Cambodian, late 19th or early 20th century

IKAT CLOTH
Silk; weft ikat. 120″ x 34½″

Bequest of Martha B. Lisle. 67.454

The Southeast Asian peninsula offers an interesting example of the persistence and diffusion of costume traditions. Most peoples of the peninsula, like both Indians and Indonesians, have worn flat lengths of cloth, draped and fastened in a variety of ways, or sewn together across the ends to form a tube like the sarongs of Indonesia. Parts of the peninsula which came under Chinese influence in the Middle Ages, however, adopted Chinese style garments like the mandarin styles found in Vietnam until the end of the 19th century. Cambodia, however, retained the style depicted in medieval Khmer sculpture, a style which has endured among many Cambodians to this day.

For the patterns of this textile, however, some foreign influence can be suspected. From at least the Middle Ages, Indian textile traders traveled by sea to Indochina and to Indonesia, and land travelers carried Indian textiles as far as China. Among the most popular of these exports were, according to Portuguese traveler Duarte Barbosa, writing about Burma in the 16th century, "printed Cambaya and Paleacate cloths, both cotton and silk, which they call patolas. These are colored with great skill, and are here worth much money."[1] Since Cambaya at the time was Gujarat's main seaport, it is probable that some of these "patolas" were the double ikat silk cloths produced in Gujarat which even now are cherished objects in Indian and Indonesian cultures. These much-admired textiles found their way throughout the Indochinese peninsula and even as far as China, Barbosa wrote.

A close examination of the subtle weft ikat patterning of this Cambodian 2/1 twill cloth confirms this probability in its design, which shows a distinct resemblance to a commonly exported Indian patola design, suggesting that local weavers took designs from the highly valued Indian textiles available to them as models, and adapted them to their own design and color sensibilities. The wonderful dark coloration of this cloth and its overall olive tones suggest that it has been overdyed, subduing the original colors. Another Cambodian ikat cloth in the RISD collection also bears a great resemblance to the Indian pattern, but its dusky pinks and dark reds again bear witness to a subtle but far from sober Cambodian palette.[2]

S.A.H.

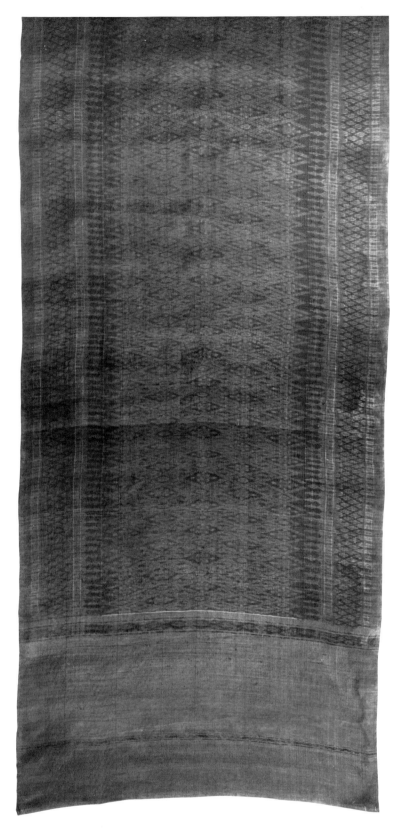

detail

1. Bühler, "Patola Influences in Southeast Asia," p. 5, quotes Barbosa from M. Longworth Dames, *The Book of Duarte Barbosa*, London, Hakluyt Society, 1921, 2, pp. 152ff, 170ff.
2. Bühler refers to this as patola motif type 25. He illustrates an example found in Bali and widely imitated there. Bühler and Fischer, *The Patola of Gujarat*, 1, pp. 106–110; 2, pl. 18; fig. 47.

28

Philippine, Mindanao, 19th century

JACKET
Abaca fiber, shell; embroidered. 13″ x 39″

Gift of Mrs. Jesse H. Metcalf. 15.235

Woven in Mindanao, the second largest and southernmost island in the Philippine archipelago, in the mid-19th century, this jacket is an example of traditional tribal design.

Although by 1830 the Philippines had been a Spanish colony for nearly 300 years, not all of its people had been affected by the outside world. Because of the rugged landscape of hills and mountains in central Mindanao, traditionalist tribesmen of the highlands escaped both Christianizing Jesuits and conversion to Islam by lowland sultans who had claimed their region since the 14th century. Their animist religion, indigenous art forms and cultural traditions survived even American occupation, but since Philippine independence in 1946 transition to more modern ways has begun and fewer indigenous forms like this jacket survive.

The jacket has been attributed to the Mandaya tribe, native to the southeastern mountains of Mindanao, because of its elaborately embroidered motifs, which include tumpal motifs so common to Southeast Asian textiles, geometric zig-zags, and a pattern peculiar to the area, diamonds containing a mazelike motif surrounded by zig-zag borders.

Often erroneously called "hemp cloth" by Westerners, the abaca cloth from which this jacket is made comes from fibers of the bark of *Musa textilis*, a kind of wild banana. It has been dyed red, probably with the root of the "sikarig" shrub, an expensive dye, suggesting that the wearer of this jacket was a person of high status.[1] It was purchased from the exhibit of the government of the Philippines at the Panama-Pacific International Exhibition in San Francisco in 1915.

S.A.H.

1. University of California at Los Angeles, *The People and Art of the Philippines*, Los Angeles, University of California at Los Angeles, 1981, pp. 123–182.

29

Indonesian, Bali, Tenganan Pegringsingan, 19th century

GERINGSING WAYANG KEBO
Cotton; double ikat, supplementary discontinuous metallic patterning wefts.
80″ x 21½″

Bequest of Lucy Truman Aldrich. 55.469

Tenganan Pegringsingan is a traditional society whose fewer than 300 members live in a walled village in extreme southeastern Bali.[1] Isolated from the rest of Balinese society, Tengananers trace their ancestry to the early inhabitants of Bali before the advent of Hinduism, value historical continuity, and conduct their lives with a great deal of ceremony.

Elaborate rituals often accompanied by dancing celebrate the stages of life from birth to death, and "geringsing" textiles, made only in Tenganan, play a large part in the ceremonies. Supposed to ward off sickness and protect the wearer from evil spirits, geringsing (whose name means "not sick") appear in the ceremony celebrating a child's first haircut, in the initiation ceremonies into the youth organizations to which all teenagers must belong, and in the wedding ceremony, among others. At the end of life geringsing may serve as a shroud, and are worn by dancers in the cremation ceremony.

Geringsing follow only five traditional patterns. They are made of cotton, handspun, dyed, and woven by women in the village. That this traditional society is changing is indicated by the fact that in the past, all women had to have the skills to make geringsing, but now only a few women weave all the geringsing produced in the village. Even with this small output, and given the fact that it may take up to eight years to produce one cloth, only the best examples are kept in Tenganan; the rest are sold to tourists both Balinese and Western.

The complicated technique of double ikat, in which both the warp and the weft threads are tie-dyed before weaving to create the patterns, is the same as the technique used to make Indian patola (cat. no. 26). Although the influence of patola is strong in some other Indonesian textiles, there is no direct evidence to show that Tengananers borrowed the technique. One type of geringsing, a design called "sanan empeg," however, shows a similarity of pattern and layout in its horizontal rows of alternating motifs to one of the most commonly exported patola designs.

The RISD geringsing is a selendang, or shoulder cloth, of the "wayang kebo" type, in which the central field is divided by a large four-pointed star or "kota mesir" surrounded by four scorpions. In the four quadrants of the field thus defined are repetitions of three figures identified with traditional Indonesian temple sculpture, particularly the reliefs of Candi Jago in East Java.[2]

S.A.H.

1. Warming and Gaworski, *The World of Indonesian Textiles*, pp. 108–114, and Bühler, Ramseyer, and Ramseyer-Gygi, *Patola und Geringsing*, passim, were sources for this entry.
2. Bühler, Ramseyer, and Ramseyer-Gygi, p. 34.

Indonesian, West Sumatra, Minangkabau,
19th century

KAIN SONGKET BALAPAK
Silk; plain weave, continuous supplementary gold patterning wefts. 90" x 40½"

Bequest of Lucy Truman Aldrich. 55.546

Perhaps the most splendid of Indonesian
textiles come from West Sumatra, where
women of the Minangkabau people weave
ceremonial cloths whose surface is entirely
covered with brocaded gold thread called
"songket."

In Indonesia cloth has never lost its symbolic function, and in Minangkabau songket must be worn by women at ceremonial
events like weddings and inaugurations of
clan leaders. The dense gold surfaces of
songket cloth represent "a woman's rich-
ness and glory," and show the importance
of women in Minangkabau's matrilineal
society.[1] Thus brides wear songket sarongs
and songket shawls. For other occasions, a
ceremonial headdress of songket folded
into the shape of "buffalo horns," the distinctive shape that echoes the matrilineal
longhouse rooflines of Minangkabau, is
worn. Since these headdresses repeat the
symbolism of matrilineality, they also
carry a message of Minangkabau ethnic
identity.

The term "songket" derives from the
term for the weaving process itself, in
which the warp threads in the loom are
lifted and a supplementary gold or silver
weft thread is passed through. This "kain
songket balapak" (rectangular cloth) is
closely woven with extremely fine gold
thread, which suggests that it dates from
the 19th century. The star-patterned
motifs are unusual, since they do not fall
into the category of most patterns which
depict in geometric form the flora of West
Sumatra. Sanday and Kartiwa theorize
that they may have come from an outside
source, since an active trade with India and
China has existed for centuries. They also
suggest that designs may have been
adapted from European pattern books that
came to Indonesia during the Dutch occupation.[2] Perhaps it is not too farfetched to
suggest the possibility that this design, as
well as the very similar design of the RISD
fragment of Naxos embroidery (cat. no.
71), may actually have come from the
same source in a European design book of
the 16th or 17th centuries.
S.A.H.

1. Sanday and Kartiwa, "Cloth and Custom in
   West Sumatra," pp. 25–26.
2. Ibid., p. 23.

detail

31

Indonesian, East Sumba, 20th century

HINGGI
Cotton; warp ikat. 96" x 50½"

Gift of Mrs. Murray S. Danforth. 38.201

On the island of Sumba, the craft of weaving is still handed down from generation to generation, and traditional motifs in design and uses for cloth continue to have significance. Hinggi are objects of wealth and status and their motifs are often symbols of royalty,[1] perhaps because historically they were worn by the kings of East Sumba and used for them as burial shrouds.[2] Because these particular warp ikat motifs are unique to East Sumba, a Hinggi worn by a man as a shoulder cloth, or a waist wrap, or both, instantly tells the place of origin of the weaver and demonstrates how traditional costume can communicate fundamental cultural information. The motifs in the RISD Hinggi can be closely related to daily life in East Sumba where the horses prominently featured in the design are important symbols of wealth and prestige.

Another motif in the cloth, a luxuriantly horned deer, is a royal symbol, because historically deer could be hunted only by the kings. The crayfish or shrimp symbolize longevity, and the confronting lions, taken from the coat of arms of the occupying Dutch, are ironically a symbol of the authority of the Sumbanese kings.[3] The fighting dogs symbolize warriors.

Hinggi are produced by women of the upper classes on a continuously warped simple frame loom, the warp threads having been arduously bound and dyed in advance. Because of the expense of the cotton and the imported dyes and the complexity of the time-consuming ikat technique, they are expensive; the wearer of a hinggi is usually a man of means and status.[4] The cloth is made in two lengths and sewn together down the middle; the design reverses in the middle so that it can be clearly seen when worn over the shoulder. The coarseness of this cloth and the indistinctness of many of the motifs suggest that it is of relatively late date and may have been made for the trade market.
S.A.H.

1. Kahlenberg, *Rites of Passage*, p. 32.
2. Warming and Gaworski, *The World of Indonesian Textiles*, p. 100.
3. Ibid., pp. 81–82.
4. Adams, *System and Meaning in East Sumba Textile Design*, p. 89.

detail

32

Tjoateengen
Indonesian, Pekalongan, 20th century

KAIN PANJANG
Cotton; batik. 99½" x 42"

Gift of Mrs. Murray S. Danforth. 49.167

In the 19th and 20th centuries, Indonesia has faced many changes which have had a major effect on the production, use, and design of traditional batik. First, Europeans introduced machine-made cotton and chemical dyes, allowing a wide range of color, and other technological changes transformed batik from a cottage handcraft into a factory manufacture. At the same time, European designs began to become popular among Indonesians as well as for export.

In one north coast town, Pekalongan, batik was produced in abundance. Located on the sea, Pekalongan felt the incoming foreign influences and was famed for immediately recognizable motifs. Here a group of "Indische" women, of European background but who had lived in the Dutch East Indies over an extended period of time, became directly involved in the traditional Indonesian arts and revived the traditional hand-drawn batik tulis. One woman in particular, Ev Van Zuylen, revolutionized the layout of the sarong and kain panjang, creating repeated graceful floral arrangements in the "badan" (body of the cloth) with birds and butterflies hovering on either side, a style which originated in Dutch botanical books and textiles that women colonists brought with them. This kain panjang, a rectangular cloth used to wrap around the body (unlike a sarong, in which the ends of the cloth join into a tube and fold around the body), shows this strong European influence.

Like Van Zuylen's designs, the bouquets in this kain are set against a clean cream ground. Van Zuylen also changed the "pinggir" (border) from strict Javanese geometry to soft scallops of alternating flowers and leaves running the entire perimeter, as seen in this kain. Another Van Zuylen preference seen in the border is flowers with colored edges and plain white petals. The large tumpal, or triangle border, on the end of the traditional kain panjang has been reduced in the manner she introduced.

The RISD kain panjang is signed "Tjoateengen," an old Indonesian spelling, probably the signature of an Indonesian batik-maker following the style introduced by Ev Van Zuylen.[1]

E.E.

1. The author thanks Robert L. Welsch, Field Museum of Natural History, Chicago, for this information.

detail

33

A. Polynesian, Tonga, 19th century

TAPA CLOTH
Pressed bark. 80" x 135"

Gift of Stephen A. McClellan. 64.122.1

B. Polynesian, Tonga, ca. 1960

TAPA CLOTH
Pressed bark. 162" x 102"

Gift of Larry Govoni. 1987.070

33A., detail

33B., detail

Polynesian bark cloth, or tapa, is fabricated from various species of trees in the family Moraceae, particularly the paper mulberry. Not indigenous to the Pacific, it was brought from Eastern Asia solely for the production of tapa. Tapa in Polynesia was once used in almost every aspect of daily life, from clothing to ceremonial rites. Today, however, it is no longer worn as clothing, and in many areas the occurrence of various traditional ceremonies has decreased sharply, reducing the use and production of tapa.[1]

The planting, cultivation, and cutting of the paper mulberry is done by men, but women assume full responsibility for the manufacturing of tapa. Pieces of bark four inches wide are dried and rolled, then stored in the rafters of the cooking house where the rising smoke discourages termites. When it is time for beating, the stored strips are soaked in water for several hours to soften, then beaten with a ribbed, flat wooden bat, which causes the bark to soften and expand as much as twenty inches.

The black and brown dyes used in the decorating of tapa are made generally by chopping and pressing the bark of various trees. Red dyes are obtained from clay. Decorating is done by repeatedly rubbing relief patterns onto the tapa. These patterns are composed by creating embroidered tablets, made from palm leaf and sewn sheath, or cords of coconut fibers and leaf midribs. Some patterns are made from carved woodblocks. Relief patterns and tablet construction vary markedly from island to island.

Before Western contact the chief's wife in each village was overseer of all tapa production, indicating its importance for social status. Today each village which produces tapa has its own guild-like organization, and a special house for the manufacturing of tapa.

The two RISD pieces, both from the island of Tonga, reveal the influence of time on tapa design. The older piece, 64.122.1, is decorated with a traditional design rubbed from an embroidered tablet. Older tablets rendered sharper relief patterns; thus the design in this piece was not painted over. It was probably used in the home as a room divider. The second, more contemporary tapa, however, was probably designed for sale to tourists. Western influence upon design composition is evident in this piece; the flagged ship and Tongan coat of arms did not appear as decorative motifs until well after the turn of the century. To increase sharpness of pattern, it was painted over with dyes after rubbing.
V.B.

1. Kooijman, *Tapa in Polynesia,* is the major source for this entry.

34

Samoan, 19th century

FIBER MAT
Pandanus leaf, feathers; plain weave.
63" x 65"

Gift of Captain and Mrs. Robert Chew.
46.495

In Samoa the term "fine mat" applies to articles which are made with the finest strips of the pandanus leaf. They are usually decorated with fringes and red feathers, as is the case in this example, and are worn as a wraparound skirt which is held in place with a belt of bark cloth. Because of the warm climate in Samoa there is little need for protective clothing. The "fine mats" were worn as personal adornment to signify rank during special ceremonies such as birth rites, weddings and funerals, and served as well as ceremonial gifts to be exchanged on important occasions.[1]

In Samoa wealth was measured by the possession of works of art, which were finely made mats and equipment for the ceremonial mixing of kava, an alcoholic beverage used by shamans or priests during rituals to achieve communication with the gods.[2] These objects were made to be passed on from one generation to another thereby assuring the persistence of high standards of craftsmanship. The mat was collected in Samoa by Captain Chew's father, a former American Governor of Samoa.

J.S.

1. Hiroa, *Samoan Material Culture*, pp. 6, 28; Terence Barrow, *Art and Life in Polynesia*, Rutland, Vermont, Charles E. Tuttle, 1973, p. 38.
2. Gathercole, Kaeppler, and Newton, *The Art of the Pacific Islands*, p. 80.

35

New Zealand, Maori, 1880 to 1890

MAN'S CLOAK
Flax, wool; twined. 77½" x 72"

Gift in memory of Mrs. and Mrs. W.
Frederick Williams, Jr. by their children.
75.026.67

The Maori, a Polynesian group, have inhabited the New Zealand Islands since the 1500s. In their original home on an unknown island in Polynesia, the Maori had worn bark cloth for clothing; the loom was unknown. Migrating to New Zealand in large canoes holding 100 passengers the Maori brought with them seeds to plant the mulberry tree, the bark of which had been used to make clothing and coverings.

But New Zealand has the coolest climate of any of the Polynesian islands, and the paper mulberry trees did not survive. Instead, between the 1500s and the time that Captain Cook first saw the Maori in 1768, twining was devised as a means of making clothing out of the native flax, *Phormium tenax*. The assumption is that the Maori were aware of single pair twining, which they used to make fish traps, transferring this knowledge to the manufacturing of cloaks.

Cloaks were embellished by adding strips of dog hair, bird feathers, pompoms of wool, fringes, and borders of densely twined geometric patterns. Men wore more elaborate cloaks than women, but it was women who made and decorated them.

Sidney M. Meade, a Maori anthropologist, has established a detailed classification of the cloaks as to types, methods of manufacture, and decoration, and the use of cloaks in Maori traditional living patterns. The fine cloak shown here, type "Heike pookinikini," was a product of the contact period. With the arrival of the British, manufactured items became available to the Maori. The women obtained wool caps from traders and unraveled them to make the black wool pompoms which are added to the twined flax body of the cloak and are typical of this cloak type. Other decorations are flax strips or "tags" dyed black and interspersed every ten inches throughout the surface of the cloak. Tube-shaped pieces of flax are also attached on the surface and a fringe made of flax which has been dyed black appears on all four sides of the cloak.

To make the cloak, warp strands of flax were attached together at the top end by a twining technique described by Meade as "casting-on." The warps hung freely and the row of attached warps were tied between two vertical weaving pegs. The weaver was seated in front of the free hanging warps and twined with weft threads horizontally progressing downward with each new row.

Traditional cloaks worn by chiefs in the early part of the 19th century disappeared relatively early. Meade explains that a main reason for this was that chiefs functioned as pioneers or leaders in change and were thus among the first to trade their garments. For this reason cloaks which were made during the latter part of the 19th century, such as this style, became very prestigious and fashionable for the Maori and much sought after by the European collector.[1]
J.S.

1. Meade, *Traditional Maori Clothing*, was the major source for this entry.

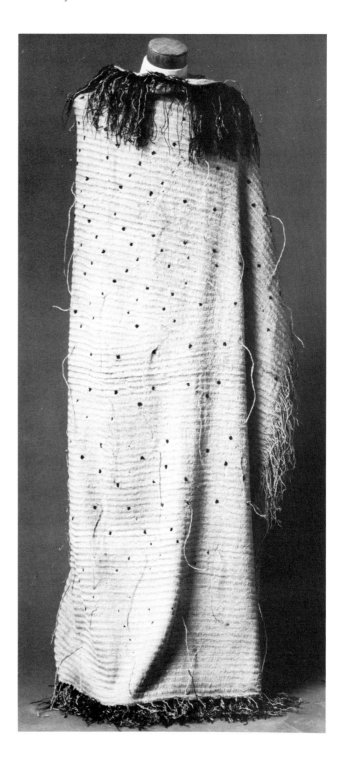

36

Chinese, 18th century

TAOIST PRIEST'S ROBE
Silk and gold paper; embroidered and couched. 48½" x 69½"

Gift of Lucy Truman Aldrich. 35.416

Publication: *Museum Notes*, 1955, p. 9.

One of the least understood of Chinese costumes, the Taoist or "Lamaist" priests' robes are also among the most spectacular.

Taoism derives from the ancient philosopher Lao Tzu (b. 604 B.C.), who believed that the heavens revolved about the earth with the Tao at the celestial pole, the seat of power. The Tao was the moving force or spirit behind the visible order of nature, and the creator of "yin" and "yang," the female and male, negative and positive principles. Over the centuries this philosophy was combined with elements of Buddhism and Confucianism into a mystical religion whose priests wore robes such as this.

The iconography of the robe reflects this combination of ideas. The central medallion has a Taoist celestial diagram with sun, moon, constellations, five mythic mountains, four gates, and cranes.[1] The body of the robe shows Buddist symbols: clouds, storks, medallions, and phoenixes, superimposed on a lattice design of couched gold thread on blue satin. The bottom of the robe is decorated with a charming Confucian universe band, with wonderful seven-clawed dragons and other animals issuing from the waves. The robe opens down the front, and was worn like a poncho.
S.A.H.

1. Vollmer, *Decoding Dragons*, p. 208, pl. 92.

37

Chinese, Ch'ing Dynasty, 1821-1850

CH'AO-FU
Silk; gauze, silk and metalic embroidery.
55¼" x 83"

Gift of Mrs. Jesse H. Metcalf. 37.043

Publication: *Handbook*, p. 145.

Although the Chinese have been wearing beautiful silks since at least the Han dynasty (206 B.C.–220 A.D.), our knowledge of Chinese textiles and costume is only fragmentary until 1644, when China was conquered by Manchu warriors from the North. The Ch'ing dynasty they founded lasted until the downfall of imperial China in 1911, and it is from this long reign that most museum collections derive their costume and textile pieces.

Instead of imposing an entirely new type of costume on Chinese society, the Ch'ing emperors for the most part adapted long-traditional Chinese garments for their own style of life. From the voluminous Manchu dragon robe, for example, which could encompass 17 yards of material, the Manchus kept the traditional dragon symbolism of imperial power and the silk from which it was made, while cutting the garment down to make it more suitable for the life on horseback they liked to lead.

The ch'ao-fu is an illustration of this fusion of Manchu and Chinese cultural elements. Vollmer points out that its cut and construction hark back to the garments made out of animal hides worn by the ancestors of the conquering Manchu, and that its shape before it is sewn mimics the pattern for best use of the leather in a skin garment. Its upper part reflected the separate riding coat of the Manchu nomads, and its tight fitting sleeve, in contrast to the wide Ming sleeve, was cut with a distinctive long or "horse-hoof" cuff which protected and hid the back of the hands. The "skirt" or double apron was practical for riding when placed over trousers. To this essentially Manchu garment the conquerors added the Chinese symbolism of the imperial dragon and other traditional Chinese motifs.[1]

The basic pattern of arrangement for the symbols in a ch'ao-fu derived from the early days of the conquest, but was strictly codified only in 1759, when a series of sumptuary laws, *The Illustrated Catalogue of Ritual Paraphernalia of the Ch'ing Dynasty* (Huang ch'ao li-ch'i t'u-shih), were promulgated by the Ch'ien-lung Emperor, regulating forms of dress for every rank and status in Chinese society. Thanks to these laws, existing garments can usually be classified by rank and the status of the wearer can be identified. This ch'ao-fu, of blue-black gauze, is embroidered with four five-clawed dragons on the

jacket, four "confronting" dragons on the waistband, and six on the skirt, a formula particular to the Emperor and his family. A blue-black color was prescribed for second and third degree princes.[2]

The remainder of the iconography of the ch'ao-fu reflects the Confucian universe: the sea at the bottom, the mountains representing the earth, a background of clouds representing the sky. The design embodies other symbols such as bats, peonies, roses and other auspicious symbols, as well as Buddhist symbols such as the "mystic diagram," sea shell, and "fish of gold," a design feature which helps to date the coat to the mid-19th century. The airy gauze fabric indicates that this was a robe designed to be worn in the heat of the summer. Because the design of the ch'ao-fu was so closely regulated, and because it was frequently used as a burial robe, it is the least common garment in museum collections today.

S.A.H.

1. Vollmer, *In the Presence of the Dragon Throne*, pp. 30–46.
2. See Cammann, *China's Dragon Robes*, for a discussion of dragon robe symbolism (pp. 77–107); also his useful appendix D, pp. 194–195.

38

Chinese, Ch'ing Dynasty, ca. 1873

CH'I-FU
Silk; gauze, silk and metallic embroidery.
55" x 75"

Gift of Lucy Truman Aldrich. 35.391

Publication: *Bulletin*, December, 1938, pp. 3–5.

Like men's formal court wear, women's clothes were also classified according to the rank of the wearer. Unlike the ch'ao-fu, which was a man's garment, women's official robes or ch'i-fu employed a simpler cut that had been used in men's robes only for semiformal occasions. Ch'i-fu could be distinguished from the robes of men because they had an extra band of brocade on the horse's-hoof sleeve, and there were two slits at the sides instead of only one at the back. Confucian cosmology was basic to the design of women's as well as men's court robes, but the symbolism of the imperial dragon was again reserved for the family of the Emperor. Color was again a distinguishing mark, yellow being reserved exclusively for the Emperor and Empress.

The RISD ch'i-fu is made of yellow gauze, embroidered not only with nine five-clawed dragons in a Confucian universe, but with twelve symbols. Many bats cavort among the clouds, and repetitions of the character "shou," meaning long life, appear in the body of the design. The robe has slits at each side and an extra ornamental band on the sleeve. The latter features, the yellow gauze, and the presence of nine five-clawed dragons all indicate that this is a summer robe of an Empress or Empress dowager.

But the presence of the twelve symbols, usually restricted to the Emperor himself, creates a puzzle if this is a woman's robe. The use of these symbols, the sun, moon, and stars for enlightenment, the mountain for protection, the pheasant for literary refinement, the sacred cup for filial piety, the fire for brilliance, and so forth, was restricted to men by the sumptuary laws of 1759. Cammann observes, however, that by the 19th century, some Empresses were being allowed to wear the symbols, as portraits and surviving documented garments prove. This robe would appear to be further confirmation of the fact.[1]

But can we pin this robe down to a particular Empress? Several design features allow a hypothesis to be made. The bats in this design are auspicious and signify great happiness; the presence of the double "shou" is associated with happy occasions, particularly weddings. The sleeves are wider than the traditional conservative Manchu horse's-hoof sleeves, but not as wide as in very late Ch'ing women's garments dating after 1875. The very wide universe band at the bottom of the robe is also a convention of mid-century. But it is the presence among the colors of the universe band of a particularly acid purple that allows a more precise date to be assigned to this robe.

In his investigations, Cammann was able to identify this reddish purple dye as Methyl Violet 2B, an aniline dye produced on a large scale only after 1866.[2] A look at the genealogy of the Emperors of the period reveals that the only Emperor to be married between 1866 and 1875 was the T'ung-chih Emperor who was married in 1873 at the age of 17. A suggestion can therefore be made that the RISD robe was made for the T'ung-chi Empress around 1873 in connection with her wedding, although we cannot be sure that it was actually a wedding garment.[3]

S.A.H.

1. Cammann, *China's Dragon Robes*, pp. 70–71.
2. Ibid., p. 63.
3. I am grateful to Maggie Bickford for the suggestion that this is possibly a bridal garment.

Color plate, page 28

39

Chinese, Ch'ing Dynasty, 19th century

COURT HAT
Straw, crystal knob, brass fittings, silk
trim. 8½″ x 13″

Gift of Mrs. Jesse H. Metcalf. 13.1470

The importance of costume as an indication of social status did not stop with the Emperor and his family, but extended through various ranks of nobility and government officialdom. Entry into the government hierarchy came about when a young man passed a qualifying examination which was open to all males. Even for these officials selected competitively, complete costumes were prescribed by the Ch'ien-lung Emperor in the sumptuary laws of 1759. The costume included a robe and surcoat of prescribed color and the requirements even extended to the form of hat worn by each rank at court. Each official wore embroidered or brocaded emblems of rank, or "mandarin squares," on his surcoat to identify his position in the hierarchy, and a button or semi-precious stone of prescribed type on the top of the hat further acknowledged his status. First degree princes (younger sons of the Emperor), for example, wore four dragon medallions on a brown surcoat, and a ruby in the hat, while fifth degree civil officials wore two mandarin squares patterned with a silver pheasant on a black or blue coat, and a crystal knob on the hat.[1]

This hat, therefore, since it has a crystal knob, must have belonged to a fifth rank official, halfway up the ladder of responsibility in the Manchu hierarchy. This hat is a summer version of the court hat "ch'ao' kuan" and is carefully constructed of several different layers of woven straw in a conical shape edged in black satin brocaded with gold, and lined with red silk gauze. It came in its own conical hat box of red leather with brass hinges.

S.A.H.

1. The information in this entry is taken from Vollmer, *Decoding Dragons*, pp. 22–25, and Scott, *Chinese Costume in Transition*, pp. 21–24 and 38–39.

Japanese, late 17th/early 18th century

BUGAKU COSTUME
Silk; damask embroidered with gold paper
and metal. Robe: 99½" x 78"; vest: 33" x
30½"; helmet: 17" x 17"

Gift of Lucy Truman Aldrich. 37.005a,b,c

Publications: *Lucy T. Aldrich Collection,*
no. 43, *Handbook*, p. 133.

When Prince Genji danced the "Waves of
the Blue Sea" in the *Genji Monogatari*
(Tale of Genji), the classic text of Japanese
secular literature written in the early 11th
century, the official Japanese court dances
known as Bugaku were at their height as a
performing art. Ordinarily performed by
official court dancers and musicians in
palaces, as well as in religious ceremonies
in the precincts of shrines and temples,
Bugaku also formed an integral part of a
nobleman's education during the Heian
period (897–1185), becoming so fully
integrated into court life that a festival or
ceremony rarely occurred without it.

Music and dance were among the first
cultural imports from Korea during the 7th
and 8th centuries, undoubtedly under the
influence of the Confucian precept that
musical harmony fostered political harmony, making it indispensable for court
functions. Additional dances were added
from the Chinese court, and although
ritual Confucian music was certainly emu-
lated, other borrowings reflected the cos-
mopolitanism of the T'ang capital, and
even Indian and Southeast Asian forms
eventually were incorporated. When these
foreign dances were collected and rear-
ranged for the new Heian court in the 9th
century, native dances were added and the
number of musicians and dancers along
with stage and costume were standardized,
and have remained so down to the present
day.

Both the ceremony and refinement of
that court culture are richly evoked by the
rare Edo period Bugaku costume preserved
in the Museum's collection, a pendant to a
similar costume that is one of the treasures
of the Kasuga Shrine, the sacred Shinto
site at Nara. Consisting of three pieces –
robe, vest and helmet – the costume,
known as "kasane-shokozu," features dark
blue, salmon, and cream as its predomin-
ant coloring. The robe ("shitagasane")
with train and reddish sleeve bands is a
white damask embroidered with a series of
blue lozenges containing flowering "kiri"
(paulownia), which are surrounded by
crests and cherry blossom sprays in a symmetrical arrangement. This broad diaper
pattern is echoed and condensed in the
sleeveless blue vest ("hanpi"), where flowering "kiri" and multi-colored birds alter-

nate. Completing the ensemble is the helmet ("torikabuto," literally "bird head
piece"), a striking green form whose high
peak and upswept apron are brocaded with
gold cloud forms; long hanging silk cords
with tassels and metal "kiri" ornaments
further enhance the formal effect. When
the dancers are assembled on stage, with
masks and accompanied by percussion and
wind instruments, the formal, stylized
movement of these colored silks progresses
in rhythmic unison, celebrating both the
sources and spirit of Japanese court life.
T. L.

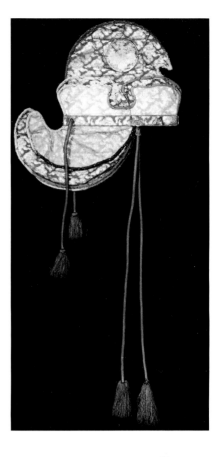

41

Japanese, 1750–1800

NOH ROBE
Silk; ikat, silk floss and metallic discontinuous patterning wefts. 55½" x 48"

Gift of Lucy Truman Aldrich. 35.472

Publication: *Lucy T. Aldrich Collection*, no. 24.

Noh is a Japanese theatrical form that evolved under strong Zen Buddhist influence during the Muromachi period (1333–1568), transforming traditional literary themes with an overlay of metaphysical meanings. Developed in the late 14th century under the direction of Kan'ami Kiyotsugu and his son, Zeami Motokiyo, Noh is the oldest major theater art in Japan that is still regularly performed. The culmination of several dance-drama forms, it encompasses a wide variety of techniques and influences that includes both temple and popular entertainments. Without patronage until 1374, when the shogun (military dictator) Ashikaga Yoshimitsu attended a performance, the popularity and refinement of Noh gradually increased, its mature form representing a sophisticated, well-balanced synthesis of dance and mime.

Performed on a bare stage with musicians and only the backdrop of a painted tree, all parts are played by men, and the use of masks is required for female and supernatural roles. Equally important is costume, which, in keeping with the flamboyance of Japan's stage and national dress, has traditionally served as a brilliant vehicle for the expression of aesthetic ideals. This example is one of many from the Museum's superb collection, considered one of the finest outside of Japan.

This "karaori," or three-harness twill robe with supplementary pattern wefts, was an outer robe worn in a female role. Its basic ground is a warp-ikat block pattern in red, brown, green, and white. On the ground is a supplementary weft pattern of a cypress fence in gold thread, while polychrome silk threads create a pattern of wisteria on the fence. The pattern of the wisteria is small in scale, there is little space between the motifs, and the weft floats are relatively short. On these technical grounds, the robe can be dated to the late 18th century.[1] It closely resembles a robe in the collection of Noh costume in the Tokyo National Museum,[2] and a robe with very similar cypress fence and wisteria is in the Tokugawa Art Museum in Nagoya.[3]

Although many of the Noh robes in the Aldrich Collection have provenance inscribed on their accompanying paper wrappers, this robe, wrapped instead in blue cloth, unfortunately came without an indication of its source.

T.L. and S.A.H.

1. Iwao Nagasaki, unpublished notes on the RISD collection, 1986, translated by Ann Morse. RISD Museum Archive.
2. Tokyo National Museum, *Noh Play Costume*, pl. 60.
3. Noma, *Japanese Costume and Textile Arts*, fig. 180.

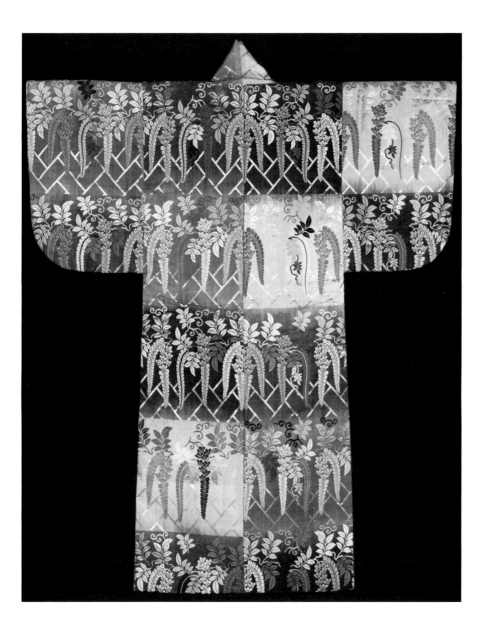

Color plate, page 29

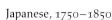

42

Japanese, 1750–1850

FURISODE
Silk; self-patterned, satin ground, twill patterning (rinzu), embroidery and shibori. 64½" x 50"

Gift of Marshall H. Gould. 46.292

In the Middle Ages, the kosode began to emerge as the favored outer garment of women of the samurai class at the Heian court in Kyoto. Once an undergarment worn with many others in the "junihitoe," or twelve-layered dress, it emerged with its narrow sleeves as a costume in its own right, and endured as a fashion for centuries, acquiring elaborate designs and wider sleeves after about 1700.[1] From at least the Edo period to the present, the "furisode," a version of the kosode with long swinging sleeves, has been worn by young women and brides.

RISD owns a set of furisode from the last half of the Edo period that includes two garments with exactly the same design, one on red figured satin (46.292), the other on white (46.289). On the geometrically patterned damask ground of each furisode are long-stemmed orchids and chrysanthemums in a key fret in alternating bands with rolls of silk and plum blossoms in shibori and embroidery, all auspicious symbols. The rolls of silk were dyed using stitched shibori, and their borders and the motifs on them were executed with satin stitch and couched gold thread. The inner decoration of the rolls includes "fawn spot" shibori, and embroidered and couched areas. The plum blossoms also belong to the "fawn spot" technique, made by tying the fabric around a tiny nailhead, creating a minute undyed circle on the cloth after dyeing. The rolls of silk resemble the decoration of a kosode in the Kanebo Textile Museum, dated to the same period, in which the large motifs are similarly uniformly scattered over the surface of the silk.[2]

These two furisode once formed a set with another furisode which would have had the same motifs, but on black silk, and formed part of a wedding costume, in which white symbolized purity, red loveliness and beauty, and black solemnity and ceremony.[3]

S.A.H.

1. Stinchecum, *Kosode*, p. 25.
2. Iwao Nagasaki, unpublished notes on the RISD collection, 1986, translated by Ann Morse. RISD Museum Archive.
3. Ishimura and Maruyama, pp. 179–180.

Japanese, ca. 1830

FURI TOME[SODE] ONSO MOYO (Design
collection of Furi Tome[sode])
Book of 25 drawings. 14″ x 10¼″ x ¼″

s49.432

Since its beginnings the RISD Museum
has had an abiding interest in collecting
sources of design as well as their expression in textiles. One result of this policy is
that the Museum today holds many design
books, ranging from 19th century American weavers' and printers' notebooks to
several Japanese design books meant for
kosode.

This book of designs for furisode, the
long-sleeved kosode worn usually by
young unmarried women, was meant as a
catalogue for customers to peruse and from
which to place their orders. Together with
drawings of designs for furisode, it contains a set of ordering instructions and a
description of the furisode. According to
its hand-written cover, it is number four
in a collection called "Kame ro Tomo," or
"Companion of the Turtle."

It would have been put together by a silk
merchant and made up of the latest designs
available. Another design book in the collection (49.430) includes patterns for obi,
and notes accompanying another (49.431)
imply that the customer coordinated her
choice of designs for kosode with other
designs of the same company for waist
sashes and other accessories.[1] Together
with many books of designs for Japanese
stenciled textiles, these books form an
unusual body of design information that
is rare among American collections.
S.A.H.

1. I am grateful to Felice Fischer, Philadelphia
   Museum of Art, for these translations.

44

Japanese, mid-18th century

KESA
Silk and gold; lampas, 2/1 twill foundation weave, 2/1 twill supplemental weave.
83½" x 45½"

Gift of Lucy Truman Aldrich. 35.276

Publication: *Lucy T. Aldrich Collection,* no. 48.

The priests and patriarchs depicted in Japanese Buddhist art typically wear a cloth of patchwork draped over their outer robes. These colorful coverings actually are religious garments called "kesa," which find their origins far to the west, in India, where Buddhism began. Indian Buddhist monks begged bits of discarded cloth and patched them together into rectangles that they wrapped about themselves and wore as religious garments. These garments, known in Sanskrit as "kasaya," were the ancestors of the Japanese kesa.

As Buddhism spread to China, Korea, and Japan, Buddhist thought and Buddhist arts responded to the different cultural and aesthetic demands of its new followers. As it took root and grew in each country, this imported religion and its outward expressions adapted to native traditions and preferences. In a typically Japanese way, kesa take the religiously prescribed patchwork wrapper as an occasion for the use of rich fabrics and strong design. Some kesa were made with patches of many different brocaded cloths, for example. But this kesa, dated to the middle of the 18th century, is made of many pieces of the same rich brocade of colored silks and gold on a black ground, with patches of a different brocade at each corner. Motifs on the kesa include crests and jui-head medallions superimposed on a lattice. In surrounding areas are the Buddhist symbols of crests, dragons, phoenixes, clouds, cranes, icons, and flaming jewels.
M.B. and S.A.H.

detail

45

Japanese, 19th century

STENCIL
Mulberry paper, persimmon tannin.
16¼" x 9"

Bequest of Isaac C. Bates. 13.557

The Museum's large and important collection of Japanese stencils came from several different donors and were some of the first objects added to the collection, ranging in date from the early 19th century to about 1914.

Stencils have been used for textile decoration in Japan since medieval times and are still in use today. First used for decorating leather armor, stencils began to be applied to textiles before the 16th century, and by the beginning of the Edo period the great Samurai families were reserving for themselves certain designs for "komon," tiny repetitive motifs such as "hailstones" or "sesame seeds" used for cotton kosode. Sumptuary laws were enacted to prevent their use by the common people, but as often happened elsewhere with such laws, stenciled pattern only became all the more coveted. As a result of this long popularity, stenciling acquired the richest vocabulary of design of any Japanese decorative technique. The stencil pictured here is only one of the enormously varied patterns in the RISD collection.

An example of extremely fine design from a time when stenciling was at its height, it probably represents a kimono design. The stencil is made of many layers of mulberry paper glued together with persimmon tannin. The stiff stencil can then be intricately cut. In the early 19th century, a length of cloth for a stenciled kimono would be spread on a long table. A resist paste of rice flour would be brushed through the stencil onto both sides of the cloth, which would then be dip-dyed, usually in indigo, and washed to remove the paste. In Kyoto, whole streets were set aside for dyehouses, which were a favorite subject for artists with their vats of indigo and strips of stenciled cloth drying in the open air.

About the turn of the 20th century, synthetic dyes were introduced from Germany, leading to the adoption of a new printing technique. Instead of using a rice paste resist on both sides of the cloth, the new dyes could be combined with rice paste, brushed directly through the stencil onto the cloth, and steamed to fix the color. This less time-consuming process also allowed more colors to be used and an elaboration of patterns followed.

Few textiles printed with stencils have survived, however, because most were printed on lightweight cotton, intended for everyday summer kimonos, underwear,

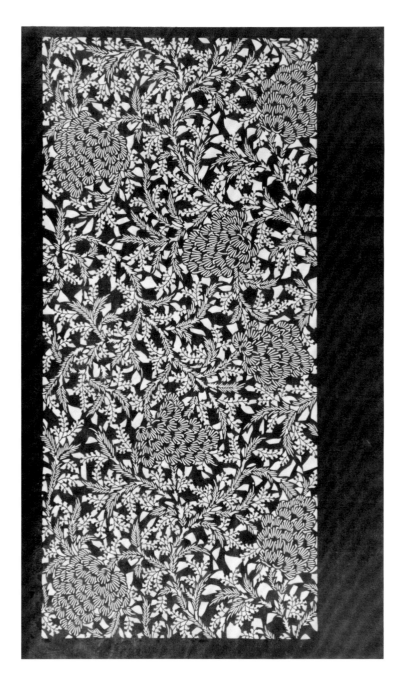

and light robes, the sorts of garments that became worn out or were not considered important enough to save. The Museum's stencils are all the more important because they provide evidence of what these lost textiles looked like. The small patterned komon continue to be printed today, and contemporary designers have revived the craft of stenciling kimono, which are now usually worn on ceremonial occasions instead of being relegated to the bedroom.[1]

S.A.H.

1. A complete account of the history of stencil dyeing is contained in the exhibition catalogue *Katazome: Japanese Stencil and Print Dyeing: Tradition and Today*.

Frontispiece

Junichi Arai
Japanese, born 1932

NUNO ME GARA, ca. 1980
Cotton; jacquard doublecloth. 117″ x 115″

Gift of Junichi Arai. 1988.040.1

Publications: Canorella, "Fabric about Fabric," pp. 72–73; Tulokas, *Textiles for the
Eighties*, p. 61.

Junichi Arai was born in the town of
Kiryu, historically known as the center of
the Japanese textile industry, in the hills
outside of Tokyo. Still located in the town
are many private weaving businesses, many
run from the home. Arai's father owned an
obi fabric company in Kiryu and his son
grew up among weavers and their art.

The knowledge which Arai gained
throughout his early exposure to weaving
is immediately recognizable in the technical virtuosity of his work, of which the
Museum has several examples. Among the
most visually astonishing is "Nuno me
Gara," or "Fabric patterned Fabric."

Arai's inspiration for "Nuno me Gara"
came from one of his previous textile
designs, a scarf based on the kente cloth of
Ghana (see cat. no. 3). Struck by the look
of the scarf as it lay bunched up, Arai
began to experiment with its design possibilities. He put the crumpled cloth on a
copy machine and began to play with the
image by enlarging and reducing it. After
he had arrived at an appropriate image, a
computer was used to generate the 3,600
punch cards needed to control the pattern
on a jacquard loom.

The fabric has a soft drape, very similar
to the folds of fabric which form its design.
It is woven with tightly twisted cotton
yarns which are starched before weaving.
The piece was washed after removal from
the loom to remove the starch. The yarns
then shrank in size, diminishing the off-
loom width of 63″ to a final width of 35½″
and giving the fabric its soft elasticity. To
make the RISD piece, three lengths of fabric were sewn together, with the seams
showing as an integral part of the design
of the hanging.
P.P.

detail

47

German, ca. 1300

FRAGMENT
Linen; twill, silk embroidery in split
stitch. 9¼" x 8"

Mary B. Jackson Fund. 47.010

Provenance: Mrs. Chauncey J. Blaire.

This small fragment, one of the earliest
European textiles in the RISD collection, is
a puzzle. Once thought to be English, it is
now believed to be of German or Swiss origin. Certainly it resembles embroidery of
similar character in Germany, in particular
the 13th century cloth of St. Ewald in Cologne and later whitework embroideries,
which use split-stitch and are organized in
vignettes. Further support is given to this
theory by its close resemblance to an early
14th century lectern cover with similar
embroidery from the convent of St.
Godehard in Hildesheim, and other Swiss
embroideries in the Abegg-Stiftung, Bern.

The Museum's fragment may have been
domestic embroidery used as a bag face or
cushion cover, or it may be a fragment of a
convent-made ecclesiastical wall-hanging
or didactic cloth. So few examples of
medieval embroidery from the German/
Swiss region survive that no other exactly
similar piece is known to exist.[1]

The horseman's costume tends to
support the idea that this is a domestic
embroidery, since his costume indicates
that he is no pilgrim but rather perhaps a
squire. The figure is isolated by a circular
border surrounded by rinceaux, a motif
that dates in textiles at least to the 12th
century and may be related to the tree of
Jesse, as in the Salzburg Cope, also in the
Abegg-Stiftung, where figures are contained within the curled branches of the
tree. The motif recurs in English embroidery and was especially popular in Elizabethan times (compare the embroidered
nightcap, cat. no. 52), when the figures
were replaced by floral motifs.
P.P. and S.A.H.

1. Our thanks to Donald King and Pat Griffiths
for their help in trying to identify this
fragment.

48

Italian, Venice, late 14th century

VELVET
Silk; cut, voided velvet. 63″ x 39½″

Museum Appropriation. 35.005

Publication: Weibel, *Two Thousand Years of Textiles*, fig. 220.

Documentary evidence shows that most of the velvets woven during the height of the Italian velvet-weaving industry in the 15th century were already in production in the 1390s, including voided velvets, polychrome velvets, cut and uncut velvets, and velvets with two and three heights of pile.[1] However, few examples of 14th century velvets exist in museum collections today, making an accurate attribution of the RISD velvet difficult. Lisa Monnas could find no surviving 14th century example of a voided velvet with a tabby ground, like the RISD piece, but the Great Wardrobe accounts of Richard II (1394–1395) list "Attabys operatus cum velvet," which, if "attabys" means "tabby," can be translated as "velvet voided on a tabby ground," and is evidence for the early existence of this type.

Other technical characteristics of the RISD piece are typical of early velvets, among them those of Lucca, where statutes dating to 1376 required that velvets be woven with a proportion of three main warps to one pile warp. This proportion was ideally suited to velvets with a plain weave ground and can be found in the RISD piece. The statutes also mention the use of inferior or waste silk in the weft; this too is found in the Museum's velvet.

Stylistically the piece relates to silks woven in Venice in the early 15th century with animals and palmettes, but the size of the pattern repeat is much larger and is more closely related to the design of the silk of a chasuble dated to the 14th century from the Schnütgen-Museum in Cologne.[2] The pattern repeat of the chasuble appears to be a similar height and width and the elongation of the bird and lion depicted on the silk is reminiscent of the RISD velvet.

Documentary evidence proves that this type of design was being produced as early as 1387, when an inventory of that date from Prague lists a textile with a design described as "lions with trees springing from their backs."[3]

P. P.

1. Monnas, "Developments in Figured Velvet Weaving in Italy During the 14th Century," pp. 69–70.
2. Mayer-Thurman, *Raiment for the Lord's Service*, p. 90, no. 18.
3. Wardwell, "The Stylistic Development of 14th and 15th century Italian Silk Design," p. 185.

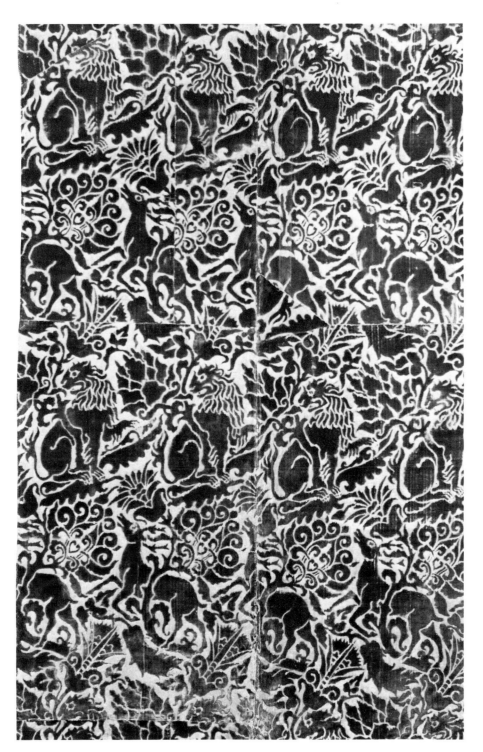

detail

detail

49

Italian, Venice, mid-15th century

VELVET
Silk; polychrome warp pile. 35″ x 23¼″

Museum Works of Art Fund. 52.110

From the 11th to the 16th centuries Venice was the center of European trade with the East, where the Venetians enjoyed exclusive trading rights with the Byzantine Empire. This brought great wealth to the Venetian Republic, which expressed itself in an active market for luxury goods, including silk. During the period from the 14th to the 16th centuries the Venetians became leaders in the silk trade, first importing silk from China, Turkey, and Persia, and eventually starting up their own industry with techniques and design elements learned from the East, forming a unique Venetian style.

Silk has been woven in Venice since the 13th century, when the first statutes dealing with its production appeared, but it was not until 1307, when an extensive migration of weavers from Lucca occurred, that the Venetian industry began to become an important producer of silks.[1] In 1347, according to documentary evidence, velvet was being woven, and in 1366, a ban on imported velvet was enacted by the Venetian senate.[2] By the beginning of the 15th century, a variety of technically advanced velvets was being woven, each type requiring special knowledge and skill. By 1451 the guild of "velluderi," or velvet weavers, had separated into five branches, each specializing in one type of velvet, including polychrome velvet like the Museum's spectacular example.[3]

The design of the velvet, two parallel serpentine branches with palmette forms, derived from Chinese, Turkish, and Persian prototypes, is typical of the 15th century, when the palmette was the major European design motif almost to the exclusion of anything else. The complicated entwined stems and the twisting leaves help to date this example to the mid-15th century. It is similar to several examples in the Museo del Tessuto, Prato.

P.P.

1. Monnas, "Developments in Figured Velvet Weaving in Italy during the 14th Century," p. 64.
2. Markowsky, *Europäische Seidengewebe*, p. 20.
3. Latour, "Velvet," p. 3455.

50

Spanish, Granada, 15th century

LAMPAS
Silk and metallic thread; 4/1 satin foundation weave, plain supplemental weave.
15½″ x 10½″

Gift of William Viall and William Dart.
19.238

Islamic arts and crafts, including silk weaving and sericulture, were brought to Spain in the 8th century by invading Muslims, and after the establishment of the Caliphate of Córdoba in 756, workshops were founded in Andalusia, Almería, Murcia, Seville, Granada, and Málaga. By the 9th century magnificent Spanish silks shot with silver threads were being mentioned in the *Liber Pontificalis*, the record of the inventories of the Roman curia.[1] Techniques and design inspiration came from the East, and early Spanish textiles depicted heraldic beasts in roundels and plant forms derived from the tree of life, patterns popular in Islamic textiles of the 9th through 12th centuries.

In 1212, much of Spain was reconquered, but the city of Granada remained under Moorish control, retaining some of the Eastern motifs and becoming the center of the silk-weaving industry, which by the 15th century ranked second behind Italy in production and influence. The silks of Granada, then the capital of the Nasrids, the last Muslim dynasty, were so coveted in Catholic Spain that prohibitions against their import were introduced.

The Museum's silk fragment was almost certainly woven in Granada sometime before its reconquest by Catholic Spain in 1492. The design of the silk shows undulating branches of palmettes crossing a crowned lion and at other times a shield, whose inscribed band was taken from the regulation Nasrid escutcheon. A plain compound satin fragment with an identical design is in the Museo de Arte, Barcelona.[2]
P.P. and S.A.H.

1. Markowsky, *Europäische Seidengewebe*, p. 38.
2. May, *Silk Textiles of Spain*, pp. 182–183; fig. 115.

51

Flemish, Tournai, ca. 1520

GRAND VERDURE TAPESTRY WITH ANIMALS
Wool; tapestry. 90″ x 137″

Special Museum Reserve Fund. 43.259

Publications: Ackerman, "A Tournay Verdure and its Asiatic Antecedents," *Studies*, Museum of Art, Rhode Island School of Design, 1947; Ackerman, *The Rockefeller McCormick Tapestries*, p. 17, pl. 32; *Museum Notes*, 1943; *Handbook*, p. 278.

Tapestries were ideal works of art for peripatetic medieval courts, since, unlike large paintings, they could be easily rolled up and carried in carts from manor to manor. By the 14th century, tapestry workshops existed in Germany, France, and Flanders to supply household tapestries for the nobility, as well as didactic tapestries for ecclesiastical settings like the "Apocalypse" of Angers or the "Life of Christ" series at La Chaise Dieu. By the early 16th century, although European courts had become more settled, tapestries were so associated with aristocratic interior decoration that they continued to be produced in quantity, many in the Flemish city of Tournai, the center of the industry at the time.

Professional tapestry weavers had been at work in Tournai since at least 1398, when regulations of the high-warp or upright tapestry looms were issued.[1] Court artists prepared cartoons for these weavings, which might depict "personages" or "histories," as English inventories referred to them, or "verdure" or "fforest work," like this tapestry.[2] This "grand verdure," also depicting animals, has been attributed by Phyllis Ackerman to the looms at Tournai about 1520, although no documentary records in Tournai can so far be definitely associated with the tapestry.[3]

Although verdure tapestries were used as wall-hangings in the most important rooms of a household, and by the early 16th century, when this tapestry was woven, often had paintings carelessly nailed on top of them, they retained something of their medieval function as didactic objects. A close look at the layout of this tapestry reveals that its subject is not simply a "fforest" but the "garden of paradise," so common in medieval painting, woodcuts, and especially manuscript illumination, with tree of life and appropriate animals. According to medieval bestiaries, still current in the early 16th century, the lion and the griffin, at the foot of the tree, were symbols of Christ and of nobility, and the heron, peacock and pheasant stood for immortality and redemption. The familiar deer peeking from behind the leaves of the tree signified the human soul seeking salvation: "As the hart panteth after the water brooks, so panteth my soul after thee, O God" (Psalms 42:1).

The animal images were taken from source books that circulated to scriptoria and secular workshops, compilations of drawings of animals, birds, and flowers which spanned the whole medieval age. The foliage in this tapestry, however, comes from no realistic drawing, and may be the oak leaves of the customary tree of life carried to an exaggerated extreme by the late-gothic artist. The "flowers" repeat forms first seen in manuscripts and in Italian decorative arts in the late 15th century, helping to give this tapestry its early 16th century date.

The RISD tapestry is closely related to another with the same layout, foliage, and animals from the Rockefeller McCormick Collection, now in the Art Institute of Chicago, and another in the Rijksmuseum, Amsterdam. Numerous others have similar "flowers," including two in the Philadelphia Museum of Art and one belonging to the Newport Preservation Society now in Marble House, suggesting that this part of the design at least was a popular one, and that the cartoons for flowers were used over and over again.
S.A.H.

1. Cavallo, *Tapestries*, p. 46.
2. Thornton, *Seventeenth-Century Interior Decoration*, p. 130.
3. Ackerman, *Rockefeller McCormick Tapestries*, p. 120; Cavallo, p. 46.

Cover

52

English, ca. 1580

MAN'S NIGHTCAP
Linen, silk, metallic thread; embroidered.
H. 10"; circumference 21½"

Helen M. Danforth Fund. 1987.042

Embroidered caps were worn by men in
England for more than a century beginning in about 1550, when embroidered costumes for both men and women first
appear in inventories. Not to be confused
with the "biggin," a cap worn to sleep in,
embroidered night caps were usually worn
on informal occasions indoors, or outside
under a gentlemen's hat. Indoors a man
might receive callers in the evening in
nightcap and gown in his boudoir, a room
which could serve both as bedroom and
reception room before the 18th century,
when separate rooms took on these functions. A Gobelins tapestry designed as late
as 1671 by Charles LeBrun shows Louis
XIV receiving in such a room seated at the
foot of his elaborate state bed hung with
silk curtains, without, however, wearing a
nightcap, a custom which seems to have
been particularly English.[1]

Most existing nightcaps in museum and
private collections repeat the pattern of the
RISD cap: stylized flowers contained in
linked circular rinceaux, but with an infi-
nite variety. None of the caps duplicate
each other in design or motifs, but one
blackwork cap with a motif of repeated
feathers has a sleeve to match, suggesting
that night caps could be part of a suit of
clothing.[2]

Where did these motifs come from? The
motif of the linked rinceaux has a long history in European embroidery, as demonstrated by the small 14th century German
fragment with horse and rider (cat. no.
47), and became especially important in
England in the middle of the 16th century
with stylized or naturalistic flowers in the
center of the rinceaux, a style that did not
seem to spread to the Continent. Women's
skirts and waistcoats, bodices and coifs all
employed the motif, as did collars, gloves,
and embroidery destined for furniture,
as many beautiful Elizabethan portraits
attest.

Flower motifs may have had several
sources, including private gardens,
medieval "sourcebooks" for flower painting, or pattern books like *La Clef des
Champs*, illustrated by Jacques le Moyne
and published in England in 1586, whose
preface indicates that it was meant for

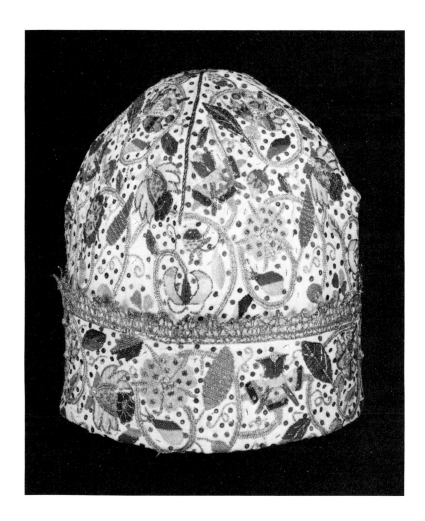

artists, metalworkers, and embroiderers.

Additional sources for embroidery patterns were the professional embroiderers
and draughtsmen who were attached to
workshops in great households like that of
Bess of Hardwick. Unfinished embroideries show the work of these draughtsmen,
who could be employed to draw patterns
for the non-professional as well.

But not all the embroidery in great
houses was professionally stitched, as Bess
of Hardwick and Mary, Queen of Scots,
who was long held a prisoner in Hardwick
Hall, themselves demonstrate. Together
and separately they produced a tremendous range of skillful embroidery including curtains, cushion covers, and other
items for furnishings, and documentary
evidence reveals that Mary worked a skirt
of crimson satin with silver as a present for
Queen Elizabeth, her jailer.[3]

In this tradition, the RISD nightcap was
probably embroidered in the household,
perhaps by a wife or fiancée. Most likely
its pattern was drawn out on the linen by a
draughtsman, or perhaps pounced out by
the lady herself from a paper pattern. She

embroidered the cap before cutting it out,
while the linen was held flat by a frame,
then assembled it and carefully added the
rich metallic lace, whose gold and silver
threads have retained their luster. Worked
in a particularly English style of decoration
and in splendid condition, it is a rare
glimpse of the Elizabethan taste for rich
display even on informal occasions.
S.A.H.

1. Thornton, *Seventeenth-Century Interior
   Decoration*, p. 13.
2. Wace, "English Embroideries," pl. 3A.
3. Digby, *Elizabethan Embroidery*, p. 57.

Color plate, page 30

53

English, 1650–1675

CASKET
Silk on linen, metallic thread, paper, mica; stumpwork, and various embroidery stitches. 11″ x 9¾″ x 7″

Museum Appropriation and Mrs. Gustav Radeke. 19.084

Publications: *Bulletin*, April 1920, pp. 16–18; *Handbook*, pp. 278–9.

From the Middle Ages well into the 19th century needlework was an integral part of the education of a young lady, an occupation that demonstrated not only her skill and patience but the fact that she was of the leisured class and could afford the time and the money to complete such work. Trained by an instructor in the needle arts, girls first executed a sampler, which was tangible evidence of skill, but could also serve as a reference book of stitches for future projects. The second project was often a small casket with embroidered panels on each side, which would be used by the girl for storage of her own small things, often including pincushions, needle and mirror cases, and perfumed sachets which she also embroidered.

The Museum's cabinet is square, a shape typical of the third quarter of the 17th century. It contains a mirror, pincushion, two bottles, a space for writing instruments, and two secret drawers. It is lined in red silk and silver paper. The four sides and the top of the casket are embroidered with silk and metallic threads in a variety of stitches suitable for a student exercise, including satin stitch, tent stitch, rococo stitch, and "stump work," then called simply "raised work." A technique common only in 17th century England, "raised work" involved the embroidery of small pictorial motifs that were then stuffed and appliquéd to the silk background as in this casket. The top of the box is also decorated with small pieces of metal and bits of mica.

On the five panels is the story of Eliezer and Rebecca from Chapter 24 of the Book of Genesis, in which Abraham sends his servant Eliezer into Mesopotamia to bring back a wife for his son Isaac. The story, a familiar feature on Jacobean caskets, is embroidered beginning on the left side of the box, the animals charmingly outlined and the figures, in the style of medieval painting, clad not in the costume of ancient Mesopotamia but in full 17th century dress. It is probable that the drawing for the Bible scenes was not undertaken by the young girl who embroidered this casket but was done for her by a draughtsman or her embroidery master. The embroidery was done before the casket was assembled; it was then returned to the cabinetmaker for completion.

P.P.

54

Italian, 17th century

BURATTO
Linen; gauze, silk and metallic thread embroidery. 10¼" x 36½"

Gift of Richard Greenleaf. 52.502

Buratto, one of the earliest types of "lace," is in reality a form of embroidered linen gauze. Together with lacis, embroidery on knotted net, it was known in the 16th century as "filet brodé," and, like whitework and raised work, was produced by domestic needlewomen. Mary, Queen of Scots, during the first days of her imprisonment, called for "des moulles et eguylle pour faire le reseau," and Catherine de Medici worked lacis, bringing designs from her native Italy to France.

Buratto and lacis had similar patterns, and inspired some of the earliest pattern books. *Il Burato*, of 1527, published in Italy, was widely used as a model for work on the woven linen ground, "buratto," that began its life as a stiff material used for sieves, but which, when made of fine linen and embroidered, could serve to make bed hangings, table covers, trim for a bodice or neckline, or, like the Museum's piece, decorative borders.[1]

The scrolling and curving acanthus leaves in formal symmetrical patterns, together with the parrots, birds, and snails in the RISD border, were from pattern books meant not for buratto alone, but for embroidery on linen cloth; they appear in samplers and other embroideries throughout Europe from Elizabethan times until the 18th century.

S.A.H.

1. Swain, *Needlework of Mary Queen of Scots*, pp.30–31; 43.

55

English, late 17th or early 18th century

JUMPS
Linen; silk embroidery. 23½″ x 25″

Gift of Nelson A., Laurance S. and David
Rockefeller, from the estate of their aunt,
Lucy Truman Aldrich. 56.078

During the 18th century women wore
stiff, boned bodices, or stays, to achieve the
desired silhouette. Stays were usually
made of linen and either full or half boned,
and gave the figure a stiff rigid line from
the chest to the waist, flattening the bust
and masking the curves in between. In
spite of the fact that stays were *de rigueur*
in fashionable society, unboned stays, or
"jumps," were often worn for undress,
during strenuous activity like riding, or by
working women. A similar French garment is defined in the dictionary of the
Académie Française of 1694 as "a small
sleeveless bodice ordinarily of quilted toile
and without bones, which women wore for
undress," and in England Samuel Johnson
defined "jumps" as "a waistcoat, a kind of
loose or limber stays."[1]

RISD's jumps are embroidered in silk on
linen in chain stitch. Examples of very
similar embroidery from the late 17th and
early 18th century exist in museum collections, including a man's waistcoat in the
Boston Museum of Fine Arts, and a similar
pair of jumps in the Costume Museum in
Bath. Common elements in these embroideries are a linen ground with overall
embroidery in silk backstitch of repeating
geometric figures, often diamonds, and
polychrome silk embroidery in chain,
stem, and backstitch of semi-naturalistic
flowers and exotic birds, perhaps indicating
that they are the products of the same
workshop or professional designer.

Among the sources of the "chinoiserie"
embroidery found on these works are
Indian embroidered coverlets which were
imported during the 17th and 18th centuries from Gujarat. The exotic birds, animals and flowers of Indian design, which
also appeared in printed textiles, served as
an inspiration for the designers of these

English coverlets and garments, which certainly were not intended to be used during
strenuous exercise or by the lower classes,
but by English aristocrats at leisure.

The jumps were purchased from the
Royal Society of Needlework in London in
1934 by Lucy Truman Aldrich.[2] Founded
in the late 19th century as a reaction to so-
called decadent forms of needlework, the
Society set out to restore to British needlework the quality it enjoyed in the 17th century by using historical examples, of which
this was probably one, as sources.
P.P.

1. Mactaggart, "Ease, Convenience and Stays,
   1750–1850," p. 41.
2. "Invoice of Purchased Merchandise" for
   Lucy Truman Aldrich, London, September
   24, 1937, Aldrich Papers, RIHS.

56

Claude Audran, designer
French, 1658–1734
Pierre François Cozette, weaver
French, 18th century

GOBELINS TAPESTRY, 1766–1789
Wool, silk; tapestry. 138½″ x 96½″

Museum Appropriation. 37.105

Publication: *Bulletin*, 26, no. 3, 1938,
p. 20.

Provenance: Sold in 1896 in Paris by the
collector Dreyfus de Gonzales.

Throughout the 18th century, tapestries
continued to be favorite wall decorations
in aristocratic settings, bearing out the
business judgment of Colbert, Louis XIV's
finance minister, who founded the
Gobelins tapestry workshops in Paris in
1662. The company was intended to provide tapestry hangings for the French
court, whether for its own use, or as pres-
ents, and many of the Gobelins products
may be followed in the records of the
Mobilier Nationale until at least the
French Revolution.

This tapestry is one of a set called
"Portières des Dieux" designed in 1699 by
Claude Audran and in production continuously until the end of the 18th century. It was woven on the "haute lisse" or
upright loom in the workshop of Pierre
François Cozette sometime between 1766
and 1789 when a reference to it appeared
in the inventory of the palace of Fontaine-
bleau together with several others in the
series: "portières de tapisserie, laine et
soie, jonquille, dessein d'Audran, mfr. des
Gobelins."[1]

Claude Audran, the designer, was the
son of Robert de Cotte, the King's
architect, and was hired by the newly
appointed Director of the Gobelins in
1699. A painter, he was a teacher of
Watteau. His designs for the "Portières des
Dieux," ordered in 1699, were a departure
from the heavy, busy 17th century
products of the Gobelins, and their classical lines and relative simplicity no doubt
help to explain their popularity throughout the century.

The cartoons for these tapestries survive
in the National Museum of Stockholm and
provide an interesting glimpse of 18th century design methodology.[2] Audran himself
first provided the composition with its general outlines and accessory decorations in
oil on paper pasted to canvas. Specialists
painted in the rest of the designs: Louis de
Boullongne drew in the figures of the gods
and the children, while François Desportes
added the animals. The borders were
designed separately, and because their
design changed over the course of the century, they are an index of the dates of the
portières, of which more than 200 examples were woven.
S.A.H.

1. Fenaille, *État Général des Tapisseries de la
   Manufacture de Gobelins*, 3, pp. 1–52.
2. Weigert, *La tapisserie et le tapis en France*,
   pp. 111–114.

57

French, early 18th century

FAN
Ivory; painted in oil and varnished.
14" x 18"

Gift of Mrs. Livingston Hunt. 31.325

Publications: *Bulletin,* April 1932,
pp. 22–23; *Handbook,* p. 280.

As functional devices, fans have been known since antiquity, and perhaps the first richly decorated fans were the ceremonial fans of ancient Egypt. Fans did not develop into objects of fashion in Europe, however, until, with the opening of trade routes to the East, Asian fans were exported to Italy in the 16th century. They are said to have been introduced to the French court by Catherine de Medici in 1549, there to become a necessary part of fashionable costume.

Two forms of Asian fan became popular in Europe: the folding paper fan, with leaves attached to sticks of ivory or wood, and the lacquered fan called "brisé," in which no paper was attached to the sticks, which were decorated and held together by a fabric border at the top. Painted and varnished fans like the Museum's were developed as a substitute for these Chinese fans by European manufacturers. The small intimate nature of brisé fans was well suited to the court of the French Regency, when the pomp of the court of Louis XIV at Versailles was replaced by small intimate gatherings of the aristocracy in their private *hôtels* in Paris.

On the obverse of the fan chinoiserie scenes surround a wedding scene in which the participants are dressed in the 18th century idea of classical garb, a suitable subject for brisé fans, which were often given as wedding gifts. Its painter is unknown, but the design, like that on a brisé fan in the Fine Arts Museums of San Francisco that is taken from Boucher's "The Abduction of Europa," probably has a source in contemporary painting or engraving.[1] A harbor scene in the tradition of Claude Lorrain decorates the reverse of the fan.

P. P.

1. Bennett, *Fans in Fashion,* p. 43, fig. 17.

obverse

reverse

58

Italian, probably Venice, early 18th
century

DALMATIC
Silk; lampas, satin foundation weave, 3/1
twill supplemental weave, continuous silk
and discontinuous gold and silver supplemental metallic wefts. 45" x 50"

Gift of Marshall H. Gould. 46.241

Publication: Weibel, *Two Thousand Years
of Silk Weaving*, p. 44, no. 332.

The generic term "cloth of gold" was in
use by the 14th century to mean any fabric
that incorporated gold in its woven structure, and might be a simple silk with a few
brocaded gold threads or a complicated fabric entirely covered in gold. Although
cloth-of-gold was used also for furnishing
fabric, much of it was woven for dress,
particularly for fine vestments for the
Church. Although ordinarily vestments
were made of luxurious silks and velvets

in colors appropriate for particular days or
seasons of the Christian calendar, vestments of gold, termed "more noble" in
Roman Catholic liturgical law, were often
worn for special occasions like Christmas
and Easter.[1]

The Museum owns a complete set of
vestments made of elaborate gold lampas,
probably woven in Venice, which dominated production of cloths of gold and
silver until Lyon replaced it as the leader
in the mid-18th century.[2] Since cloth of
gold was exported all over Europe, however, it has been impossible to determine
the place of manufacture of the vestments
themselves.

The pattern of the silk dates to the early
18th century, when the "bizarre" style
came to dominate silk design. This style,
which was given its name descriptively in
the 1950s, has puzzled scholars with its
abstract, curious patterns depicting fantastic fruits and flowers, sometimes combined
with small realistically drawn but eccentric
objects such as archways or even furniture
forms. Because the flowers and fruits are
reminiscent of the exotic flora of Indian

chintzes, and the objects are often related
to Chinese decorative art forms which
were just beginning to be fashionable in
Europe, it is likely that the inspiration for
these silks is Eastern, but no documentation exists to prove this theory.

The silk in the RISD vestments shows a
form of the "bizarre" probably dating to
about 1710. Columns in the warp direction
are entwined with wholly abstract, ribbon-
like forms and large, fanciful flowers and
fruits, including what Natalie Rothstein
has called "belted tennisballs." The RISD
silk is heavy and stiff, probably indicating
that it was made specifically for vestments
rather than as dress material.[3]
P.P. and S.A.H.

1. Aidan Kavanagh, "Liturgical Vesture in the
   Roman Catholic Tradition," in Mayer-Thurman, *Raiment for the Lord's Service*, p. 14.
2. Natalie Rothstein, "The Elegant Art of
   Woven Silk," in Maeder, *An Elegant Art*,
   p. 74.
3. Ibid., p. 79.

59

French, ca. 1725

LACE
Linen; needle lace. 4¼″ x 22½″

Museum Appropriation. 25.020

The French lace industry, built up during the 17th century by Louis XIV and his Finance Minister Colbert, suffered major setbacks at the beginning of the 18th century when light muslins imported from India made the heavy needle lace of the 17th century unfashionable. Bobbin laces made in Flanders benefited from this change in fashion, because the bobbins with which they were made could be used to weave a background much like, but even finer than, the imported muslins. In France, the lace industry attempted to adjust to fashion by creating backgrounds of lightweight mesh rather than emphasizing the pattern motifs, or toilés, which in the late 17th century had heavy raised edges and stiff, large motifs. Because French laces were made with a needle, using fine buttonhole stitches, the light effect was more difficult to obtain than in bobbin lace, and lacemakers developed a variety of lightweight backgrounds.

The design of this border, varying from sprays of exotic flowers and fans to scrolls and a fanciful palm tree and including background motifs of differing geometric figures, are taken from contemporary textiles called "lace patterned silks," a design type popular in the 1720s and 1730s. Contrary to the implications of this name, applied to the silks by much later observers, stylistic evidence suggests that it was the laces which imitated the silk patterns, and not the other way around. The feathery palm tree motifs and the elongated "gourds" in this design, together with the variety of background motifs, are typical of the period. The RISD border is similar in design to a number of pieces in the Victoria and Albert Museum.
S.A.H.

60

French, Lyon, mid-18th century

CLOTH OF GOLD
Silk and metallic thread; taffeta, discontinuous patterning wefts. 51" x 21½"

Gift of Marshall H. Gould. 46.256a

French manufacture of cloths of gold seems to date from the mid-17th century, when an entry of 1666 in the Journal of the Royal Garde-Meuble, founded by Colbert to keep inventory of the furnishings of Louis XIV's residences, referred to rolls of silk from Lyon "brocaded in gold and silver on both sides."[1] From this time onwards, cloths of gold appeared regularly in the inventories for the decoration of the Hall of Mirrors in the Trianon, for the Grande Galerie at Versailles, for the King's "Cabinet de Curiosités," and in the 18th century, for the royal residences at Compiègne and St. Cloud as well as at Versailles.

But cloths of gold and silver were also used for dress, as the Garde-Meuble records attest: in the second half of the 17th century the manufactory of Marcelin Charlier supplied gold and silver cloths "to dress the King."[2] Further proof is the existence of these two fragments, dating from the 18th century, which once formed the back panels of a "robe à la française," the gown most often seen at French court balls.

The dress had a fitted front bodice with a loose back hanging free to the floor from a set of double box pleats, and an open front under which a matching petticoat was worn. The skirt was extremely full at the sides, held out with side hoops or panniers. RISD's lengths are pieced together from smaller fragments and the original shape of the back panels of the dress can be traced. The pieces also retain the folds where originally they formed the double box pleats of the upper back.

The design of the silk is typical of the 1750s and 1760s, with lace-like serpentine meanders of ribbons or flowers climbing up the textile. Parallel branches with naturalistic carnations and apple blossoms sprout from the same stiffly arranged stems.

Woven into the silk are gold strip (lamella), gold and silver lamella wrapped around a silk core (filé), and gold lamella wrapped around a silk spiral core (frisé). In design and technique it is closely related to many examples of the same date in the Musée Historique des Tissus, Lyon.
P.P. and S.A.H.

1. Quoted in *Silks from the Palaces of Napoleon*, n.p.
2. Ibid.

detail

61

French, 1760–1770

DRESS
Silk; cannelé, discontinuous supplementary patterning wefts. Center back length: 59¼"

Gift of the Museum Associates in honor of Eleanor Fayerweather. 82.287.1a–c

Publications: *Museum Notes*, 1983, p. 16; *Handbook*, p. 281.

The style of women's 18th century dress was established late in the 17th century and in its most popular form came to be known as the "robe à la française." In three basic pieces, its largest component was an overdress that opened down the front, its loose back held in double box pleats at the back of the neck. This hung to the floor forming a train in the back. The front of the bodice was held together with a stomacher, a triangular piece of fabric usually elaborately decorated. Beneath the overdress a woman wore a petticoat, which was exposed by the open front skirt.

Foundation garments supported and shaped the dress, in particular the stays which gave the bodice a stiff hard line, and garments were often fitted to the stays instead of the figure. To support the skirts of the dresses women wore panniers, wire or whalebone cages which were worn on either side to extend the hips. The cut of the gowns was based on the width of the silks, about 21 inches. Because 18th century silk was extremely expensive, the gowns were constructed so that cutting into the fabric could be minimized, using only a few shaped pattern pieces in the bodice. Most shaping was created by pleating the silk, which showed it off to its best advantage in the wide expanse created by the panniers and the double box pleats of the back of the gown.

The basic style of 18th century dress remained the same throughout the century with yearly changes in fashion reflected in the fabric, trim, and proportions of the gown. The relatively small size of the panniers of the Museum's gown, the meandering ribbon pattern of the fabric, and the delicate trim date it to the third quarter of the 18th century when the "robe à la française" was beginning to go out of fashion. Cottons imported from India, which were again readily available after the ban on their importation into France was lifted in 1759, began to replace heavy silks, and dress styles began to adapt themselves to the lighter fabrics, fitting more closely to the body. Cotton dresses were reserved for undress, or informal wear in the home, but "robes à la française" like this one were still worn for formal occasions, such as balls, the opera, or court functions, their proportions slimmed down following the fashion of the new cotton gowns.

RISD's dress, unlike many that survive, still retains its petticoat and its stomacher, and its overall superb condition makes it a fine example of French dress of the 1760s.
P.P.

62

French, ca. 1760

MAN'S SUIT
Silk; velours miniature. Length: jacket,
42"; vest, 27"; breeches, 25¼"

Gift of the Museum Associates in honor
of Eleanor Fayerweather. 82.287.2a–c

Publications: *Museum Notes*, 1983, p. 16;
Handbook, p. 281.

The origins of the man's three-piece suit
go back to the second half of the 17th
century. At that time men abandoned the
doublet and jerkin and began to wear
matching knee breeches, coats, and vests.
This ensemble continued to be worn
throughout the 18th century until the
beginning of the 19th when long trousers
replaced knee breeches, creating the three
piece suit which men continue to wear
today.

In the 18th century men's dress suits
were often as elaborate as women's dresses,
made of expensive silks and beautifully
embroidered with silk and metallic threads.
The Museum's suit is of floral patterned
velvet, a cloth commonly used for winter
suits.

Because of their elaborate design, men's
suits were made by tailors, unlike women's
gowns which were left to the dressmakers
because of their simpler construction.
Since the suits were tailored to the body,
greater numbers of more complicated pattern pieces were required. Because of the
profusion of pieces involved in the construction of a suit it was often easier to
embroider the pieces before they were put
together. This same principle is used in the
construction of the Museum's velvet suit.
As the velvet was woven the shape and
ornamentation of each piece, including
decorative borders, was delineated in the
patterned velvet. When the velvet came off
the loom the pattern pieces were cut out
and the suit assembled with the ornamentation in place. Velvet with small figural
ornamentation was known as "velours
miniature" and was produced only in
Lyon, where thousands of samples still
exist in the Musée Historique des Tissus.[1]

This suit and a similar one in the Victoria and Albert Museum can be dated by
the small stand-up collars on the jackets, a
feature which was popular in men's formal
suits of the 1760s.
P.P.

1. This information courtesy of Jean-Michel
   Tuchscherer, Museum of Fine Arts, Boston.

63

English, Spitalfields, ca. 1747

COVERLET
Silk; liseré and discontinuous supplementary patterning wefts. 89″ x 79″

Gift of Barbara Deering Danielson.
82.308.39

Throughout the 18th century the French silk industry, especially that of Lyon, dominated the European silk trade both in quality and design. Other European countries, including England, had their own industries but spent most of their time trying to keep up with the ever changing French designs. It was not until the mid-18th century that the English industry acquired a design repertoire of its own and the ability to compete with French silks.

James I had begun the English silk industry early in the 17th century hoping to obtain some of the profits which were enriching the Italian silk weavers of Florence and Venice. French weavers were invited to settle in London, and, by the

reign of James II, the industry was well developed, although English silk could still not compete with silks made in France. During James's first year on the throne, Huguenot refugees, many of them accomplished weavers, began to settle outside of London in the district of Spitalfields, as they fled France after the revocation of the Edict of Nantes in 1685. Here a thriving silk industry was firmly established during the War of the Spanish Succession (1701–1713), when French commerce went through a major depression. Because of the shortage of French silks, domestic demand for the silks of Spitalfields increased along with their export as luxury goods to both Ireland and North America. By the 1740s the English were providing high quality goods, both skillfully woven and with fashionable patterns. The development of Spitalfields silk patterns during the mid-18th century can be traced thanks to the survival of many of the original designs.

Early 18th century English patterns show an increasing naturalism, a result of reaction against French designs, which were labeled by some as "tawdry tinsel" and having a "glare of colors."[1] The profusion of flowers depicted in these silks can be closely associated with botanical prints, part of the English fascination with gardens and newly imported plants. This naturalistic style dominated Spitalfields silk designs until the last part of the 1740s, when the emphasis switched to the background of the silks and the variety of flowers represented dropped. The textiles of Spitalfields became more and more stylized during the 1750s and 1760s, when, because of competition from the imported cottons then becoming fashionable, the industry went into a decline from which it never recovered.

The design of this silk is typical of Spitalfields silks of the late 1740s. The ground of the fabric is self-patterned with undulating ribbons in a technique known by the French term of liseré, in which the design is created with the main warp and weft. A pleasing dialogue is set up by juxtaposing the ground with the supplemental patterning of roses created by the brocading wefts.
P.P.

1. King, *British Textile Design*, 1, p. xxv.

detail

64

French or Italian, mid-18th century

CHASUBLE
Silk; plain weave with supplementary patterning warps, embroidered in polychrome silk and metallic threads. 43½″ x 28½″

Museum Works of Art Fund. 46.507

The chasuble, the outermost garment worn by the clergy, was often the most elaborately decorated, and church law dictated that chasubles be made out of silk, the most expensive of materials.[1] During the Middle Ages and through the Renaissance chasubles and their orphrey bands were often embroidered with pictorial scenes, most often from the Bible. In the Middle Ages these pictures served as didactic tools, and in the Renaissance, many were designed by or after important artists like Pollaiuolo or Andrea del Sarto.

In the 17th and 18th centuries, the design vocabulary of vestments changed, becoming less didactic and more decorative, with less religious symbolism. Chasubles might be made of silks originally designed for aristocratic dress and given to the Church by its supporters, or, as in this example, embroidered in the naturalistic floral style so popular in mid-18th century woven silks, a style that reflected the new interest in nature, gardens, and botanical illustration.

The opulence of clerical dress is, however, still reflected in the elaborate use of gold thread. A gold strapwork frame is created around the flowers by the use of a variety of metal threads, including frisé, filé, lamella, and paillettes. The fiddleback front and small size of the RISD chasuble, which differs so greatly from the large, cone-shaped form of the Middle Ages, also help to date it to the mid-18th century.
P.P.

1. Mayer-Thurman, *Raiment for the Lord's Service*, p. 28.

Color plate, page 31

65

Attributed to Heinrich Ollbrich
German, Saxony, 18th century

NAPKIN, ca. 1750
Linen and silk; damask. 43½" x 37"

Museum Works of Art Fund. 50.295

The weaving of linen damask appears to date from the early 16th century, and in Flanders was centered in Courtrai, which became the leading weaving center. German Saxony also was a weaving center. Since flax was grown in eastern Saxony, fine thread was available, and in the 17th century weavers came from Flanders to establish the industry there.[1]

By the 18th century the area was producing extremely fine damasks of linen and, as in this napkin, of silk and linen, supplying the courts of Saxony, Prussia, Poland, and Russia. Damask made in Saxony still has a reputation for fineness and whiteness in France, and in England it was so coveted that a trade barrier was set up in the 18th century to protect Irish and Scottish weavers.

The rococo decorations on this napkin were certainly inspired by the artistic revival taking place in nearby Dresden, where the Electors of Saxony invited French and German artists to redecorate the old palaces in rococo style, and established an academy of painting under the Frenchman Louis de Silvestre. German artists frequently went to Paris to study, returning to work for the German courts. Perhaps Heinrich Ollbrich, whose designs the napkin embodies, was one of these.[2]

The design of the napkin depicts the god Apollo, surrounded by the four continents, Asia, Africa, Europe, and America, as well as the four elements air, water, land, and fire, all decorated with wonderful rococo feathers and curious chinoiserie. It is identical to napkins in the Abegg-Stiftung, Bern, and in the Cooper-Hewitt Museum, New York.

S.A.H.

1. Prinet, *Le Damas de Lin Historié*, pp. 96–97, has a discussion of the history of damask-weaving in Saxony.
2. Information on notecard of this napkin from the Abegg-Stiftung, Bern.

66

Jean-Baptiste Huet, designer
French, 1745–1811
Christophe Philippe Oberkampf, manufacturer
French, 1738–1815

LOUIS XVI RESTAURATEUR DE LA LIBERTÉ, 1791
Cotton; copperplate printed. 41″ x 37½″

Gift of Francis C. Whitehead. 69.136.5

An Englishman, Francis Nixon, working in Drumcondra, Ireland, was the first to discover that copperplates could be used to print mordants or dyes onto cotton or cotton and linen, creating large textiles of great beauty in monochrome colors of red, blue, purple, or brown. Nixon took his method to London, where copperplate prints took over the top end of the furniture market and became a coveted item of export to the American colonies. Other English printers adopted the method, and particularly fine copperplate prints were manufactured by Robert Jones at Old Ford, the factory of Bromley Hall in Middlesex, and by Francis Nixon himself in Phippsbridge near Merton, Surrey.

Christophe Philippe Oberkampf, a Swiss emigré, founded a factory for blockprinting on textiles at Jouy, near Paris, in 1759, becoming in a decade the most successful printer in France. But even he was ignorant of the new English technique until a trip to London in 1769, when a visit to Old Ford convinced him of the desirability of trying to manufacture copperplate prints himself at Jouy. But blockprinting remained the mainstay at Jouy until 1783, when Oberkampf had the good fortune to hire Jean-Baptiste Huet, a court painter, to design copperplate textiles. Over the next 30 years until Huet's death in 1811, some of the finest copperplate prints in existence were produced at the Jouy factory and acquired for Oberkampf a reputation for quality that assured the firm's survival through the Revolution and revival under Napoleon.

In 1788, Oberkampf ordered from Huet a cartoon for a textile entitled "Triomphe de la Royauté," a subject itself drawn from a textile printed in Manchester about 1780 entitled "Homage to George III."[1] In the cartoon, Louis XVI on the throne, confronted with supplicant figures representing the citizens of France, grants them religious liberty, holding in his hand the balance of justice. Beside the king stands a figure of Religion, a great cross in her hand. When the textile finally went on sale in 1791, the figure of Religion had been changed into a classical figure of Liberty, with liberty pole and Phrygian cap, an interesting example of how even textile printers had to scramble to keep up with political events. The textile after its alteration from the original cartoon was entitled "Louis XVI Restaurateur de la Liberté," and judging from its continuing production over three years, was clearly a popular subject.

It was produced by applying a mordant to the surface of the copperplate which was retained in the engraved lines. A piece of cotton cloth which had been extensively sun-bleached and calendered to make its surface as smooth as possible was then placed on the printer's table, where the copperplate was applied with a press. When the textile was placed in a dyebath of madder, the engraver's design emerged printed in reverse on the textile. This method, although time-consuming and expensive because of the skill needed to prepare the plate and to print it successfully, had the advantage of being able to produce very large and impressive images, limited only by the size of the plate and the width of the woven cotton, images that were popular among the wealthy for furniture covers and bed hangings.

S.A.H.

1. Chassagne, *Oberkampf*, p. 152.

67

Dubern et Compagnie
French, Nantes

COPPERPLATE PRINT WITH POLYCHROME
DECORATION, ca. 1790
Cotton; plain weave. 76" x 34¼"

Gift of Francis C. Whitehead. 69.136.08

Although copperplate printing produced textiles with very large repeats and very fine line drawing, the technique was limited because of the size of the printing plate. Since the plates were so large, it was virtually impossible to print in more than one color, because the difficulties of getting another plate to register exactly with the first were insurmountable. Most plate-printed textiles were thus monochromatic, using red, blue, brown, or purple against the bleached white of the cotton or cotton and linen cloth.

Some printers in Nantes, however, developed a technique in which the outlines of the design were printed with a copperplate in black or brown, and the details were block-printed or penciled in, in polychrome. This textile was printed about 1790 at the factory of Dubern and Company in Nantes. A signature, or "chef de pièce," was printed on the end of each bolt, according to French law; this piece is an end-of-bolt length with the words "Manufac de Dubern-Fils A Nantes Bon Teint" (referring to the fast color of the dyes) printed at the bottom.

Like wallpaper, this textile was meant to hang vertically on a wall; it has no repeat and was printed as a single panel, probably requiring several copperplates to achieve its length.

The buildings in the central medallion recall the ruins of Rome, with the Colosseum and the Pyramid of Caius Cestius. The ornaments are the same as those in the wallpapers of Reveillon of about the same date.[1]
S.A.H.

1. Jacqué and de Bruignac, *Toiles de Nantes*, p. 140.

68

Philippe de LaSalle
French, Lyon, 1723–1805

WALL PANEL, ca. 1785
Silk; taffeta, supplementary discontinuous
patterning wefts. 100″ x 29¾″

Gift of Francis C. Whitehead.
69.136.54a,b,c

Philippe de LaSalle, working during
the second half of the 18th century, was
perhaps the greatest of the Lyon silk
designers. Like other important designers
who worked in Lyon during the 18th century, de LaSalle was trained as a painter,
studying with Daniel Sarrabat in Lyon,
and Jean-Jacques Bachelier and François
Boucher in Paris. He was persuaded to
return to Lyon by the designer and manufacturer Charryé, for whom he began to
design silks. During his later association
with the famous workshop of Camille
Pernon, he was commissioned to design
textiles for Catherine the Great and Marie
Antoinette among other contemporary
figures. Although only a few of de
LaSalle's designs still exist, and only a
handful of records from the date of the
RISD piece, the firm, which still exists as
Tassinari and Châtel, retains accounts of
all the largest orders from the end of the
18th century onwards.[1]

De LaSalle's style in this piece reflects
the taste of the French aristocracy in the
last decades of the 18th century. In this silk
he continues the pastoral themes so popular during the reign of Louis xv, but in a
more sentimental vein; he uses trophies
depicting elements associated with the
idyllic life of the country shepherd, such
as the pipes, tambourine, shepherd's cap,
and bagpipes, instead of the aristocratic
themes of earlier trophies, like music, war,
or the hunt. The organization of the pattern around a medallion of nesting birds
reflects the advent of neoclassical taste,
and the birds themselves are a reflection of
the aristocratic yearning for the country
epitomized in Marie Antoinette's Petit
Trianon and "Le Hameau," a miniature
country village built for her at Versailles.

The panel would have been used like
wallpaper in the furnishing of a room,
composing part of a suite of room furnishings, in an ensemble with coordinating bed
curtains, upholstery, and, if present,
window curtains. The room for which this
fabric was commissioned is unknown at
present, but two mises-en-cartes exist in
the Musée Historique des Tissus in Lyon
of a similar fabric by de LaSalle for the
Salon de la Reine in the Trianon.[2]

The piece is technically extraordinarily
complex, demonstrating not only the
superiority of silk design in Lyon but the
adaptability of the newly improved draw
loom on which it was woven. Using a combination of various yarns and bindings, de
LaSalle created not only a complicated
pictorial image but also one of contrasts in
texture and light. Both silk floss, which
reflects the light, and silk ondé (spirally
twisted yarn), which has a matte finish,
were used as brocading threads. To add
further texture to the piece, de LaSalle
employed a variety of binding weaves,
including twill and "cannetillé," in which
short ribs arranged in horizontal blocks
give the appearance of small monochrome
checks in the background of the piece.
P.P. and S.A.H.

1. Jean-Michel Tuchscherer, "The Art of Silk,"
   in Carlano, *French Textiles*, p. 69, n. 22.
2. This information courtesy of Marie-Jo de
   Chaignon, Lyon.

69

William Kilburn
Irish, 1754–1818

DRESS, ca. 1790
Cotton; plain weave, block printed. Center
back length: 68″

Helen M. Danforth Fund. 1987.028

In about 1788, William Kilburn began to
paint the 233 watercolor drawings which
compose an album of his designs for cotton
prints now in the Victoria and Albert
Museum. Renowned in England as one of
the best calico printers of his day, Kilburn's
textile designs in this album proved to be
some of the most colorful and complex
ever drawn. As late as 1985, however, no
actual textiles by Kilburn were believed to
have survived. Just before this dress was
purchased by the Museum in 1987, its
design was shown to be from the Victoria
and Albert album, identifying it as by
Kilburn and dating the fabric between
1788 and 1792, the dates of the album's
drawings.

William Kilburn was born in 1754 in
Dublin and trained there as a textile
printer. His primary talent, however, lay
in drawing patterns and designs for
blockprinting, and once he arrived in England following his apprenticeship his
designs for London printers were immediately successful. In the 1770s, he turned
to botanical illustration, producing elegantly drawn plates for William Curtis's
Flora Londinensis, the first botanical
treatise which attempted to illustrate every
plant growing in the environs of London.
His experience in botanical illustration
clearly served him well, since his reputation continued to grow, and in 1792, now a
factory owner himself, his patterns were
praised as "perhaps the nearest approaches
to nature in drawing," including flowers,
fruits, shells, ribbons, and seaweed. It was
a seaweed pattern like the RISD dress, an
expensive pattern which sold for a guinea
per yard, that he gave to Queen Charlotte,
wife of George III, for a gown.[1]

It is sometimes difficult from the van-
tage point of the 20th century to imagine
that cotton prints such as this were among
the most expensive textiles available, and
for good reason. Each design required the
exact cutting of perhaps 50 different
woodblocks, one for each detail, one for
each color. Cotton cloth perhaps imported
from India was first bleached, then
mechanically calendered between rollers
to flatten it as much as possible. The red,
black, and brown details were printed onto
the cloth using a different chemical for
each color. The cloth was then dipped in a
bath of madder dye, again imported from
India, and washed and dried to reveal the
patterns printed on the white cloth. A fast
yellow dye had been invented by this time,
but together with the details in indigo, it
still had to be separately brushed on. A
final washing and drying were required
before the application of the finish, which
still appears on the RISD dress.

The style of the dress fits well with the
dating of the textile; the dress was probably made when the textile was brand new
and at its most fashionable, around 1790.
It has a bodice with square neck, pointed
in front and at the center back. At the
point of attachment in the back are narrow
gathers that give the dress the shape fashionable for 1790, when padding was
strategically placed to create a softly bus-
tled, flowing line. Silk tape decorates the
edge of the sleeves and one side of the
dress. The dress may originally have had a
matching petticoat; however, white muslin
petticoats were also often worn.
S.A.H.

1. Victoria and Albert Museum, *Rococo Silks*,
   pp. 7–8.

70

Mills Junr.
English, London

CORSET, ca. 1795
Cotton; silk embroidery. 12″ x 35½″

s1987.092

In contrast to the early 18th century, when
dress shapes changed very little, French
fashion evolved rapidly during the reign of
Louis XVI. Marie Antoinette's simple white
muslin gowns became the fashion for
informal wear at court while for formal
court functions the grand habit with stif-
fened corps and full panniers was still
required. About 1780 fullness in the skirt
began to be gradually eliminated at the
sides, and moved to the back, supported by
soft padding rather than the stiff panniers
of court gowns (cat. no. 61). Armholes
were set back into the shoulders drawing
further attention to the back. After the fall
of the Bastille marked the end of court
fashion, the waistline began to rise. By
1794 its height became extreme enough for
the newspapers to comment on it,[1] and a
small "corset" began to be worn to give the
correct line. These developments were
imitated throughout Europe and in England, showing what little effect political
events had on French leadership in fashion.

In the RISD corset, made in London,
the armholes are cut back into the corset
with the shoulder straps cut tight in the
front to draw the shoulders back. The corset
has its own small pad attached, positioned
high on the back, marking the waistline
and supporting the fullness of the skirt at
this point.

The corset is stamped with a maker's
mark; "Mills Junr., 34, Holywell Street,
Strand, London., Inventor of the Patent
Telima Corset." "Mills Junr." had been in
business since at least 1804 when he placed
an advertisement in the *Norwich Mercury*
for "Elastic Corsets which expand to every
part of the shape."[2] Because the Museum's
corset has casings for boning but no elastic,
it probably dates to the late 18th century.
The Telima corset, which Mills claimed to
have invented, took its name, like many
other fashions of the time, from the Greek.
P. P.

1. Madeleine Ginsburg, "Barbara Johnson and
   Fashion," in Rothstein, *A Lady of Fashion*,
   p. 25.
2. Mactaggart, "Ease, Convenience, and Stays,
   1750–1850," p. 48.

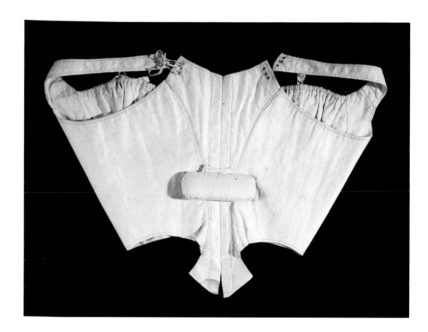

maker's mark

71

Greek, Cyclades, Naxos, 18th century

CUSHION COVER
Linen; silk embroidery. 24½″ x 24½″

Gift of Miss Elizabeth D. Bugbee. 18.184

A tradition of embroidery on linen for domestic needs has existed in the Mediterranean since at least the first centuries after the birth of Christ, as many exquisite surviving embroideries prove. From Western Asia to North Africa, all the regions of the Mediterranean coast have changed hands frequently, but each region has a traditional style of embroidery that has persisted over several centuries in spite of changing foreign influences.[1]

The Cyclades in the Aegean Sea were part of the Byzantine empire until its partition in the 13th century, when they were attached to Venice and were ruled from Naxos, the largest and wealthiest island, and the source of this textile. In 1566 the islands were conquered by the Turkish Ottoman empire and were held until the Greek War of Independence in 1823 won

the islands for mainland Greece. In spite of, or perhaps even because of, this turbulent history, traditional customs and behavior survived in the Cyclades well into the 19th century. Folk traditions of embroidery persisted with very little change from at least the 17th to the 19th centuries in each of the islands, so that surviving fragments can be assigned by style to their origin.

All the Cycladean islands had a common tradition of domestic architecture which dictated the forms textiles took. One-room houses had a hearth at one end, with a raised sleeping platform at the other, which was curtained off and decorated with embroidery on the wedding day and on all feast days thereafter by the woman of the house, who had spent many hours embroidering bed curtains, valances, cushion covers and towels.[2] As a symbol of wealth and of status, embroideries were collected by wealthy families over the generations. Even as late as 1884, an English traveler remarked that island families retained great stores of embroidery, some of which

dated back to Venetian days.[3] In later years, the craft of embroidery died out, and many of these treasures were cut up and distributed as smaller fragments to the daughters in the family.[4]

This cushion cover from Naxos is in reality an assemblage of several fragments of embroidery sewn together, perhaps as a result of such a distribution of family pieces. The fourpointed star design of the larger fragment has occurred nearly without variation in Naxos since at least the 17th century. Technically the embroidery is a simple darning stitch worked in the same shade of red silk. The apparent variation in color occurs because the stitches are worked side to side in one area and up and down in another, so that light is reflected differently from different parts of the design. Trilling traces this motif to a design for 16th century French lace.[5] The lower part of the cover incorporates two fragments in a small-scale geometric pattern, again created by reversing the direction of the stitches. The whole is surrounded by borders sewn on separately, together with a linen fringe.

S.A.H.

1. Stone, *The Embroideries of North Africa*, illustrates many examples of these forms, each in their own traditional patterns.
2. Polychroniadis, *Greek Embroideries*, p. 17.
3. J.T. Bent, *The Cyclades*, London, Longmans Green, 1885, pp. 340, 368.
4. MacMillan, *Greek Islands Embroideries*, n.p.
5. Trilling, *Aegean Crossroads*, pp. 30–32.

72

French, early 19th century

COURT TRAIN
Silk; velvet, embroidered with silver
lamella. 132″ x 63″

Gift of Mrs. Harold Brown. 37.215

Provenance: Mme Henri Gratien Bertrand; left to her daughter Mme Amédée
Thayer; willed to the Marquis de Biron;
acquired by Harold Brown.

Publications: Christopher Monkhouse,
"Napoleon in Rhode Island. The Harold
Brown Collection at the Rhode Island
School of Design," *Antiques*, 113, no. 1,
January 1978, pp. 192–201; *Handbook*,
p. 284.

Costume played an important role in establishing the regal atmosphere of Napoleon's
court, and the emperor took great interest
in seeing that the ladies of the court wore
the opulent, classically inspired gowns that
expressed the great role he envisioned for
France. For formal occasions, simple white
gowns were heavily embroidered and often
studded with gems, and long trains, made
of velvet and heavily embroidered with
gold and silver, were worn over the gowns
for the most formal occasions. Trains had
been an essential part of court dress during
the 17th and 18th centuries, and Napoleon
quickly adopted this royal symbol as an
important part of his court etiquette.
Court trains played a prominent role in
both his coronation in 1804 and later in his
marriage to Marie Louise in 1810, as etch-
ings of the ceremonies by Percier and
Isabey attest.

The provenance of the RISD train can
be traced back to Mme Henri Gratien
Bertrand, whose husband, a general in
Napoleon's army, was an intimate of the
emperor and accompanied him on his
Egyptian campaign; with his family, he
was with Napoleon on both Elba and St.
Helena. According to information provided
by the donor of the train, it was worn by
Mme Bertrand at Napoleon's coronation.
Although this is possible, it is more likely
that the train was worn in 1810 for the
marriage of the emperor to Marie Louise.
At the time of the coronation Bertrand's
position was only that of an aide-de-camp,
while by the time of the marriage he had
attained the rank of general. Supporting
this theory is a similar red velvet train in
the Costume Institute of the Metropolitan
Museum of Art, which, according to its
history, was worn for the marriage ceremony, although the embroidered design of
the RISD train is not exactly the same. In
what was certainly a planned idiosyncracy,
Mme Bertrand's train is encircled with
Egyptian palmettes, making a personal
reference to Napoleon's Egyptian campaign, where his friendship with Henri
Bertrand began.
P.P.

Color plate, page 32

73

Cléambault
France, Alençon

BED COVER, completed 1809
Linen; needle lace. 90" x 75"

Edgar J. Lownes and Mary B. Jackson
Funds. 42.001

Provenance: Stolen from the Tuileries in
the 19th century; acquired in the 1880s by
Mr. Biddle; sold to Warner S. McCall, 1929.

At the end of the 18th century the French
Revolution made the wearing of lace, long
a symbol of aristocracy and wealth, not
only unfashionable but politically danger-
ous. At this time the number of lacemakers in Alençon dropped from 6,000 to
500, and remained at this low ebb until
Napoleon came to power. In his plan to
revitalize the French economy Napoleon
spoke of commissioning many works from
the manufactories which formerly supplied
the monarchy, among them lacemakers
from Alençon. But most of the lace bought
by Napoleon and his court continued to
come from Brussels, and the commissions
made in France were never entirely suc-

detail

cessful. The Museum's bed cover provides
an example of how Napoleon's commissions frustrated the lace manufacturers in
Alençon rather than supporting them.

While Josephine was married to
Napoleon, a bed-set was commissioned for
her use at Malmaison. The order was
handled by M. Deschaleries of Paris and
the bed set was made by the firm of Cléambault in Alençon. It consisted of curtains,
valances, canopy, and a bed cover, decorated with symbols typical of Napoleon.
The ground of the bed cover is sprinkled
with bees, which Napoleon considered to
be the symbol of his empire, saying they
were "evocative of nationhood. Bees were
found in the tomb of Childeric I. The
insect is the symbol of industry. The stars
will be for me, the bees for the people."[1]
The reference to Childeric (the father of
Clovis, the first king of France) refers to
the more than three hundred gold bees
which were found in his tomb, and which
for Napoleon evoked the great nation he
hoped to establish.

It is ironic that this commission, made
to help the Alençon lace industry, had just
the opposite effect. In the year in which
the coverlet was completed, the year
of Napoleon and Josephine's divorce,
Napoleon refused the commission and it
remained in the hands of Deschaleries. In
an attempt to get Napoleon to purchase the
bed set for his new wife, Marie Louise,
Deschaleries had Josephine's monograms
removed from the set, and in some pieces
replaced with those of Marie Louise. The
four corners of the RISD bed cover show
oddly shaped patches attached with threads
coarser than those used when the coverlet
was originally pieced together. Probably
in an attempt to cut his losses Deschaleries
chose in this piece to replace Josephine's
monograms not with those of Marie
Louise, but with patches continuing the
ground of the bed cover. Marie Louise
eventually persuaded Napoleon to purchase the bed set, but for a price much less
than the actual cost of production.

Technically the bed cover is a superb
example of Alençon needle lace. Close
inspection reveals that it is made of small
sections of lace about 6" x 8", which
were individually made, and then finally
assembled.

Sections of the valance are in the
Brooklyn Museum and the Cooper-Hewitt
Museum in New York; the canopy is in
the collection of the Toledo Museum, and
the two bed curtains are in the Brooks
Memorial Art Gallery in Memphis,
Tennessee.

P.P.

1. *Silks from the Palaces of Napoleon*, p. 35.

74

Attributed to John Marshall
English, Manchester, early 19th century

ROLLER-PRINTED FABRIC
Cotton; plain weave. 73¼" x 20¾"

Gift of Mrs. Jesse H. Metcalf. 28.100

Again in the early 19th century, it was the English who took the lead in originating new printing technology. Invented in the 1770s, but not widely used until the turn of the century, roller printing began to replace copperplate printing in English factories as a new middle class market began to emerge. By the 1820s the center of the English industry had moved from the environs of London to the Midlands and particularly Lancashire, where John Marshall was printing at 19 Spring Gardens in Manchester between 1818 and 1824. Peter Floud identified in 1957 a group of related textiles some of which were signed by Marshall, and which are so similar that they have been assumed to have been made by him around 1820. One of these is this textile, printed in red on narrow machine-woven cotton, with a very shiny "chintz" finish.[1]

Although the subject of this textile is in doubt, the figures must, like other examples that have been identified, be drawn from print sources, possibly illustrations of popular literature or songs. The design of the textile, however, can be directly traced to a French source, a copperplate-printed textile printed in about 1810 by Favre Petitpierre et Compagnie in Nantes entitled "Les Bergers Ecossais," an example of which in blue is in the Musée de l'Impression sur Étoffes in Mulhouse.[2] This textile has the same scenes as the RISD textile, but the RISD print has the scenes reorganized and compressed to fit into the much narrower width of the machine-woven cotton.

The textile was printed by engraving the design onto a copper roller about 19" in circumference attached to a machine, applying mordant to the roller, and rolling the cloth through. The piece was then dyed in madder, finished, and polished. Another roller-printed textile with some of the same scenes was described by Floud, and attributed to an Alsatian printer.[3] Undoubtedly this textile and the RISD textile are examples of a common phenomenon, in which printers pirated designs at will or copied parts of them from earlier textile patterns which had already proved their merit in the marketplace.

S.A.H.

1. Floud, "English Printed Textiles VII," p. 458.
2. A textile with this title appears on a list, "Noms des Dessins pour Meubles," published by Petitpierre et Compagnie in 1810. Jacqué and de Bruignac, *Toiles de Nantes*, p. 101, fig. 75; p. 155.
3. Floud, p. 459, fig. 10.

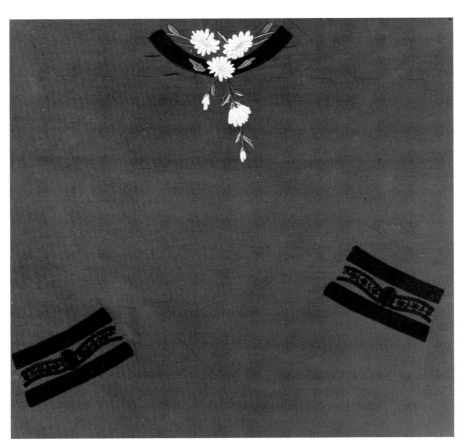

detail

French, ca. 1862

UNMADE DRESS LENGTH
Silk; silk and jet embroidery.
13¾ yards x 26½"

Gift of Arthur B. DuBois, Mildred H. Rutter, Carl DuBois, and Rebekah DuBois Glazebrook. 83.193.4

The Museum's unmade dress length, or ready made dress, gives a glimpse of dress manufacturing techniques during the mid-19th century. In this 13 yard piece of taffeta, the silk has been embroidered prior to its being cut and sewn by the seamstress, a technique that had been in use at least since the 18th century, when the elaborate construction of men's waistcoats and some men's suits necessitated that the pieces be embroidered before being cut out and sewn (see cat. no. 62). The outline of the pattern pieces was traced onto the length, in these days before paper patterns, allowing an accurate reconstruction of the gown to be made.

Embroidered dress lengths were sold in England as early as 1845 when "sewed muslin," unmade dress lengths embroidered with white work, were advertised. In the 1860s the same technique was applied to silk garments as an "Ornamental Design for a Complete Dress to be Sold as One" registered with the Board of Trade in London in 1861 shows.[1] The placement of the embroidery of this dress is similar to that of the Museum's length, on the collar, cuffs, bodice center front, underskirt front, and the open front of the overskirt.

The Museum's French silk length probably dates to the same period as that of the dress registered with the London Board of Trade. During the early 1860s, ladies' magazines show a decided preference for the color purple, along with a growing use of embroidery to trim gowns. This gown, when the pattern pieces were sewn together, had an open front and underskirt showing below, a style that was fashionable during this time, and resembled the gowns of the 18th century, a period of which French Empress Eugénie was especially fond.
P.P.

1. Levitt, "Registered Designs," p. 57.

Color plate, page 33

76

Alexandre Buquet, designer
French, Rouen, 1825–1894
Ernest Renault, printer
French, 19th century

MOUCHOIR D'INSTRUCTION MILITAIRE
NO. 2, 1875
Cotton; plain weave, engraved roller-
printed center, block-printed border.
29" x 29"

Gift of Constance Wharton Smith.
58.165.12

Commemorative handkerchiefs had been a part of the printer's art since at least the early 18th century. Political figures and events were the usual subjects of these pieces, but an English copperplate printed handkerchief of about 1785 in the Museum's collection shows a detailed map of England, Scotland, Wales, and Ireland. A handkerchief of this type is documented by an inventory of 1787 to have been in the possession of John Brown, Rhode Island's wealthiest merchant.

Commemorative handkerchiefs remained popular throughout the 19th century, and in the 1830s the Buquet family began a prolific career designing them for a number of printers in the Rouen area, in subjects ranging from Napoleon's tomb to the marriage of Napoleon III and Empress Eugénie.[1]

They were printed on cotton usually in red or blue, and white with black, with the "illustration" roller-printed in black in the center of the blockprinted border. The Buquet studio would engrave the copper roller for the process. The rollers, up to about 19" in circumference, which were first used for machine printing about 1830, were used over and over again. This meant that the engraver first had to sandpaper off a previous design; this is the reason why so few engraved rollers exist in museum collections today. The engraver then used a tiny burin to emboss the new design into the soft copper surface. The printer used his machinery to print this design in black and white, finishing the handkerchief by hand blockprinting the border. This handkerchief was printed by Ernest Renault of Darnetal, outside Rouen, a manufacturer who bought Buquet designs from 1870 until the closing of the atelier in 1903. Because the scarf is dated 1875, we can be certain that its engraver was Narcisse-Alexandre Buquet, whose father and brother had died in the 1860s and who worked alone in the 1870s until his nephew and son were old enough to assist him.

Some of the Buquet patterns were strictly commemorative, destined for a collection of such pieces or for display as wall decorations. Some were repeat patterns that could be used successfully as neck scarves, and were also produced as yardage. In the case of the "mouchoirs d'instruction," however, we may be deal-

ing with an educational rather than a purely commemorative textile. Two other Buquet patterns seem to fall into the same class. They are a square printed with 32 useful household recipes, and "le medicin dans la poche," a guide to first aid which, as its name indicates, could be carried along in the pocket for instruction in first aid if needed.

Were the "mouchoirs d'instruction militaires" a kind of take-along textbook for soldiers? It seems apparent that their function must have been more that of patriotic symbol than useful object, for, as the hole in the corner of this handkerchief may indicate, the soldier who had to rely on his handkerchief for directions in handling his gun had been trained too little, too late, and the field of battle was no place to learn. Probably these handkerchiefs were meant to serve as commemoratives of the soldiers in the field during and just after the Franco-Prussian War, when most were printed, and were entrusted to family members as mementos.

"Mouchoir d'instruction militaire No. 2" contains instructions for taking apart and putting together the 1874 model French army rifle. Drawings around the edge show proper behavior for a sentinel in many different situations.
S. A. H.

1. Brédif, *Les Mouchoirs Illustrés de Rouen au XIXe Siècle*, was the source for this entry.

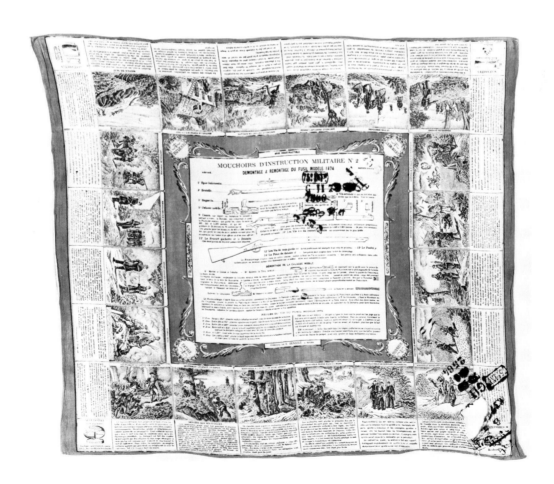

77

Charles Frederick Worth
English, worked in France, 1825–1895

DRESS, ca. 1895
Silk; satin and tulle, embroidered. Center
back length: bodice, 10″; skirt, 71″

Gift of Mrs. C. Oliver Iselin. 62.021.1a,b

Charles Frederick Worth began his career as an apprentice for Swan and Edgar, silk mercers, on Regent Street in London, and later moved to the more fashionable Lewis and Allenby, purveyors to Queen Victoria. During these years Worth gained a thorough knowledge of textiles and the textile trade and eventually decided to take that knowledge to the center of fashion, Paris. After acquiring a knowledge of the French language and of the French textile market, Worth began working for Gagelin, one of the most fashionable silk mercers in Paris, in the outerwear department. Here, shop girls, or "demoiselles de magasin," were employed by the firm to model the shawls and mantles for customers. Worth

began to design simple gowns for his favorite model, Marie Vernet, whom he eventually married. Customers soon began requesting these gowns, and eventually Worth formed his own dressmaker's shop on the Rue de la Paix.

With the help of one of the most fashionable women of Napoleon III's court, Princess Pauline von Metternich, Worth's gowns came to the attention of Empress Eugénie herself. The publicity gained when she became one of his most enthusiastic clients launched him as the arbiter of taste, a position he retained for more than 40 years.

To Worth, the textiles he used dictated the cut and drape of the gown. The connections he developed with textile manufacturers while working for Gagelin gave him direct contact with the silk mills of Lyon, and he was able to commission special fabrics, giving a boost to the silk industry while gaining him the support of Napoleon III. Worth's patronage also spread to lacemakers and passementiers, whom he kept busy with his innovations in dress trim.

Worth found unlimited inspiration in museum collections, where he drew ideas from historic costume depicted in portraits. RISD's dress, with its "slashed" sleeves, looks back to Renaissance costume, a period Worth often drew upon in his later designs, and dates to about 1895. Since this was the year of Charles Worth's death, there is a possibility that the gown might have been designed by his son, Jean Charles, who with his brother Adolph took over the house after their father's death. But the Renaissance inspiration of the bodice and the plainness of the satin skirt which sets off the impressively beaded front panel are typical of Worth's later designs, and suggest that this gown is a product of the master himself.
P. P.

May Morris, designer
English, 1862–1938
Dame Alice Mary Godman, embroiderer
English, died 1944

CUSHION COVER, ca. 1890
Linen; silk embroidery. 26½" x 26"

Farago Art Fund. 85.200

Publication: *Museum Notes*, 1986,
pp. 18–19.

Designed by May Morris, youngest daughter of William Morris, during the later years of Morris and Company's operations, this linen pillow cover is embroidered in a pattern called "Tudor Rose" using vegetable-dyed shades of apricot, red, green, and yellow plied silk on a turquoise ground.

Typical of Morris embroidery, it is executed in satin and running stitches that accentuate the design without themselves making distracting patterns. Morris chose to stylize form and allow the luster of the silk yarns to predominate; he abhorred the naturalism, so popular during the 19th century, that the technical freedom of embroidery could easily allow. A master dyer, Morris obtained colors from medieval herbs, believing that textiles of "aesthetic quality" could not be produced from the coal-tar-derived aniline dyes that were in common use by the middle of the 19th century.

First used as a means of tying together and completing his experiments in interior design that developed at his own "Red House" in 1859, embroidery became a particularly important vehicle in Morris's attempt to raise the decorative arts from the minor status they had assumed in the 19th century. Embroidery's rightful place, he felt, was alongside the major arts of tapestry and painting.

In the early days, the firm's embroidery was executed by Morris's wife, Jane, the wives of the other artist associates, and wives of clients; as a consequence it was often a matter of several years before some Morris interiors could be considered complete. By 1870, the intimate circle of embroiderers had expanded to become a professional workshop, with increasing responsibility being taken by May, Morris's younger daughter, who started helping her mother embroider tapestries at age seven. By 1885, May ran the embroidery division of the firm alone. Outside of her work for the firm, May herself had an interest in promoting an appreciation of embroidery and of "women's art." In 1907, she helped to found the Women's Guild of Art, which was described as a "centre and bond" for women who were doing decorative work. By the 1890's, cushion covers had become an item of popular commercial success for Morris and Company. They could be purchased either complete for a relatively small sum or as kits in varying stages of completion for even less. Since the running and satin stitches that were used varied in direction, the execution of an embroidery kit engaged both the mind and hand of the embroiderer and in the process achieved Morris's dream of a true partnership of designer and craftsman working with equal skill and creativity.

The maker of this piece was Dame Alice Mary Godman, second wife of Frederick Du Cane Godman of South Lodge, Lower Beeding, Horsham, Sussex, according to an accompanying label. Frederick Godman was a trustee of the British Museum and a prototypical Victorian "amateur" interested in all aspects of natural history. He toured Central America to study and collect natural history specimens, and wrote a monumental volume, *Biologia Centrali Americana*, in 1916. His important collections of Iznik, Hispano-Moresque and Persian pottery were eventually left to the British Museum.

His wife, Dame Alice, is described as an "explorer and keen shot." She was a Commissioner of the Girl Guides and won a British Empire Medal for her contribution to the British Red Cross during World War I, later becoming a Deputy President of that organization. A second label attached to the cushion cover indicates that Dame Alice won an award and was named an Associate of the Royal Amateur Art Society, in part because of her skillful and artistic execution of May Morris's embroidery design.

J.I.O.

79

Liberty and Co.
English, London, founded 1874

COAT, ca. 1913–14
Silk; jacquard. Center back length: 49"

Gift of Candis Dixon. 1987.067

Publication: *1900 to Now*, pp. 38, 128.

Liberty and Co. opened its doors in
London in 1874 showing designs based on
Japanese art and the Aesthetic Movement.
These included a wide range of the decorative arts, especially textiles and later costume. The costume department was added
in an attempt "to establish the craft of
dress making upon some hygienic, intelli-
gible, and progressive basis uninfluenced
by the ateliers of Paris."[1] Like the members of the Aesthetic Movement, Liberty's
was interested in making women's dress
more comfortable and practical, and in
loosening the restrictive nature of late 19th
century dress. As a model, the firm looked
back to the costume of the Middle Ages.

This coat is an excellent example of the
Liberty style; the peacock-feather fabric is
based on an early design by Arthur Silver
of 1887, a style identified with Liberty's to
this day. The coat is a "cocoon," a style
that was popular circa 1913–14, just before
the outbreak of World War I, and was part
of the vogue for orientalism which occurred in Europe with the coming to Paris of
the Ballets Russes in 1911. At the same
time, a trace of the medieval influence so
common in the costume of the late 19th
century can still be found in the Museum's
coat in the "faux" hood and tassel which
hang down the back, a common element
in Liberty costume. One of Liberty's most
popular evening cloaks was "the Burnous,"
an example of which is also in the RISD collection, whose most eyecatching element
was just such a hood, decorated with a
huge silk tassel.
P.P.

1. Arwas, *The Liberty Style*, n.p.

Mariano Fortuny y Madrazo
Spanish, worked in Italy, 1871–1949

DRESS, 1933
Silk; pleated plain weave and stenciled velvet. Center back length: 63"

Gift of Mrs. Lucy T. Wormhoudt. 73.013

Son of a gifted painter, Mariano Fortuny was a man of many talents, painter, inventor, scientist, photographer, and craftsman. However, it is not Fortuny's paintings, drawings, or inventions which live on, but his pleated Delphos gowns and his beautifully stenciled fabrics. He considered his dresses to be not "fashion" but works of art, and devoted as much energy to them as to his paintings and photographs, having a hand in every stage of their production. He drew his inspiration from the arts of the past, from classical Greece and Rome, the Middle Ages, and the Renaissance, and owned a collection of historical textiles.

The Museum's dress, bought in 1933 at the Palazzo Fortuny in Venice, might date from any year during his career in costume design. Fortuny's interest in dress began with one basic concept, the Delphos gown, and variations of a scarf or jacket worn over it. The Delphos gown was patented in Paris in 1909 along with the pleating technique now so closely associated with his work. He then created other models, like the Museum's gown, combining the pleated silks of the gowns with the stenciled velvets used in many of his jackets.

The Museum's dress is in the style of a medieval tabard with a silver-stenciled velvet panel in the front and back, inspired by Hispano-Moresque textiles made in 13th and 14th century Spain. Between the velvet panels are pleated silk inserts, and holding the front and back panels together are silk cords attached to the back panel with Venetian glass bead buttons. The dress combines many techniques used by Fortuny, and is an example of how his garments, inspired by the past, were produced using new technologies which he developed.

Fortuny's method of pleating has been a mystery since his death. It was probably done by hand, while the fabric was wet, and heat-set using a machine patented in 1909, which consisted of a series of heated porcelain or copper tubes through which the silk was undulated. The combination of heat and moisture under high tension set the pleats while the undulating motion of the tubes created the uneven, changeable quality of Fortuny's pleats.

The dress is also an example of Fortuny's method of stencil printing. His inspiration was Japanese stenciling, which he adapted to create a forerunner of modern silkscreen printing. Stencils made of laminated silk were soaked in gelatin and the design outlined using a chemical solution either manually or photographically. When exposed to light these areas would become insoluble, and when the stencil was washed, would remain on the silk to create the desired design for printing.[1]
P.P.

1. De Osma, *Mariano Fortuny*, was the source for much of the information in this entry.

81

Marie Louis Suë
French, 1875–1968
André Mare
French, 1885–1932

FURNISHING TEXTILE, 1912–1917
Silk; damask. 37" x 26"

Helen M. Danforth Fund. 1987.006

Provenance: Mme Vène, daughter of
André Mare.

Art Deco, or Art Moderne, as it was called in its early days, emerged as a coherent movement in 1925 at the Exposition Internationale des Arts Décoratifs et Industrielles held in Paris, which included an important pavilion called "Un Musée de l'Art Contemporaine" with works by the Compagnie des Arts Françaises of Louis Suë and André Mare. Suë, an architect, and Mare, a painter, began their collaboration in 1912 at the Salon d'Automne with a small exhibition called "La Maison Cubiste." Cubist in the sense of "modern," it had less to do with the abstractions of Cubist painting than the sense of simplicity and boldness applied to traditional forms that were characteristic of early Art Deco.

The same year Suë and Mare formed their first architecture and design firm, "l'Atelier Français." Espousing the unity of the arts both architectural and decorative, they believed that the design of buildings should be carried out as a whole, from the construction of the façade to the upholstery of the furniture. Suë would produce the architectural drawings; Mare, together with artists and craftsmen Maurice Marinot, Jacques Villon and others he had assembled at "l'Atelier Français," would produce the decoration of the interior, with the design of every object under their control.

Decorative arts objects would then be produced with attention to traditional French decoration but in a modernist style. As in the late 18th century, baskets of fruits and garlands of flowers were to be important motifs and indeed would serve as the symbol of the new decoration, but they would be drawn with a new simplicity and boldness of line and form.

After the closing of l'Atelier Français during the war, Suë and Mare again took up the thread, founding the Compagnie des Arts Françaises in 1919 on the same principles. Immediately they attracted important commissions, including the design of the French Embassy in Warsaw and the home of couturier Jean Patou.

By the late 1920s, however, the influence of Cubist painting had begun to take hold in decoration and an interest in abstraction, straight lines, and austerity of form had begun to prevail over the traditionalist orientation expressed in the designs of Suë and Mare. The Compagnie des Arts Françaises lost favor and ceased production in 1928.

This textile is perhaps a quintessential expression of the Suë and Mare philosophy. Into a traditional heavy red silk damask, the designers have woven a bold yet simple rendering of the basket of fruit that was the symbol of their early collaboration. Proof that the textile dates to 1917 or before is the signature woven into the selvedge, "l'Atelier Français."[1]

S.A.H.

1. I am grateful to Judith Applegate for much of the information in this entry.

detail

82

Paul Poiret
French, 1880–1944

EVENING COAT, ca. 1925
Silk; satin, hand-painted velvet. Center
back length: 44½"

Gift of the Estate of Edith Stuyvesant Van-
derbilt Gerry. 59.031.3

Paul Poiret has attracted the attention of
scholars and the public in recent years as
one of France's most eccentric and possibly
most original designers. Born in Paris in
1879, he began drawing dresses in 1898,
and by 1899 was in the employ of Jacques
Doucet, who had inherited Worth's mantle
as the leading couturier in Paris. Later, in
the studios of Jean Worth, the Grand Master's son, his designs were dismissed as too
bold for the public. Poiret opened his own
salon in 1903 and designed for such clients
as Josephine Baker, Colette, and Peggy
Guggenheim.

Poiret's own life was often as large as
those of his clients; he entertained at legen-
dary parties, for which he designed grand
scenery as well as lavish costumes, partici-
pated in and designed for the theater, and
even created a nightclub in his own back
garden. His wife Denise was the inspiration
and model for some of Poiret's most famous
designs of this period: the lampshade dress,
which he designed for her to wear to the
"Thousand and Second Night" party he
gave at his house in Avenue d'Antin in
1911, and the harem dress, designed for
another soirée. Poiret counted among his
friends many painters and other artists,
including Matisse, Dunoyer de Segonzac,
Dufy, Picabia, and Derain. He believed
that "couture is an art" as much as any
other, and should reflect new trends like
Symbolism and Fauvism.[1] Instead of
employing classically trained design assis
tants, Poiret opened his "Martine" school
to train young women of no particular
background in designing whatever patterns
they could imagine, having been instructed
by Dunoyer de Segonzac, Dufy, and other
friends of Poiret in drawing flowers, fish,
and modernist country landscapes.

This evening coat designed by Poiret
about 1925 reflects Poiret's interest in
painting and particularly in modernism. A
perfect example of his evening dresses for
1925, "a beautiful drapery of velvet unrol-
ling around a straight column of silk," its
most striking features are the hand-painted
velvet scarves which envelop the shoulders
and fall across the bodice.[2] The scarves,
signed by Renée Vautier, a young sculptor
and interior designer, seem closely related
to designs by Kees Van Dongen, the Fauve
artist who often painted elongated nudes
cavorting in the forest, like the scenes
on the scarves. Van Dongen was a close
friend of Poiret who taught in the Martine
school, and several of his works hung on
the walls of the Poiret house. The painting
"Quietude," 1918, now in a private collection, which hung in the Poirets' bedroom,
had nudes arranged in attitudes closely
resembling those on the scarves.

Although Poiret's popularity decreased
in the 1920s and led to the failure of the
house in 1926, this coat is one of his finest
designs.
S.A.H.

1. Deslandres, *Poiret*, p. 106.
2. *Le Bon Ton*, 9, 1925, p. 422.

Color plate, page 34

83

French, ca. 1917

FLIGHT SUIT
Cotton; twill, fur-lined. Center back
length: 62½"

Gift of Mr. and Mrs. Peter J. Westervelt.
81.134

Publication: *Museum Notes*, 1982, p. 11.

Prior to 1910, there was little need for
special flying clothing. Aviation was in its
infancy and aircraft were still too fragile
and unreliable for sustained high speed or
high altitude flight. Everyday suits, sports
clothes or motoring garments were worn
for flying. Woolen underwear, goggles
and perhaps a short leather flying coat or
cotton overalls provided adequate protection against wind, cold and engine oil.

By 1910, aviation was popular enough
that several companies (among them Bur-
berry's) produced flying outfits and padded
"crash" helmets. These garments were the
starting point for the research and development of flying clothing which began in
earnest during World War I.

At the beginning of the war, airplanes
were usually in the observation corps, to
gather information on enemy troop move-
ments. Their potential as weapons was
gradually exploited, but not until the
introduction, in late 1915, of the propeller-
synchronous machine gun did the airplane
become a significant offensive weapon.
Each side worked to develop aircraft capable
of flying higher and faster than the oppo-
sition. As speeds and altitudes increased
and more reliable engines allowed for
longer flights and operation in less than
perfect weather—but still in open cockpits—
the need for more effective rain and cold-
resistant clothing became obvious.

The design of the French one-piece
flying suit illustrated here is typical of
flying clothing from 1916 until well into
World War II. The durable cotton twill
shell is completely lined in fur and has
wrist and ankle straps to tighten against
drafts. The suit was usually worn over the
standard service uniform. Several pairs of
gloves and socks, helmet, goggles and
heavy boots completed the outfit, although
individual aviators added long underwear,
sweaters, balaclava helmets and scarves for
additional warmth. The "Sidcot Suit,"
used by British fliers after 1916, had an
additional silk interlining and pockets
placed on the lower thighs. Electrically
heated suits were introduced in 1916, but
they were generally unreliable, and the fur
lining was retained as backup.

Post-1918 winter and high-altitude suit
designs included experiments, usually by
the military, with materials such as fur or
blanket-lined leather, down-filled quilted

fabric and shearling. Diagonal zipper
closures and multiple pockets are also post-
war characteristics. Two-piece suits, which
gave better fit, were in use towards the end
of the 1920s.

This suit, although French, was worn
in 1917 by an American aviator, Captain
Stephen Perry Jocelyn, a member of the
16th Infantry who was assigned to the Air
Service in 1917 as an aerial observer. Use
of French equipment was not at all unusual.
The United States entry into World War I
in April 1917 had caught the Quartermaster
staff as unprepared as the rest of the military. Since Americans had already been
serving with the French Air Service in the
Lafayette Escadrille, French-made garments continued to be procured for use by
the Air Service of the American Expedi-
tionary Force.
M.S.

84

Italian, Pellestrina, early 20th century

LACE COLLAR AND CUFFS
Silk; bobbin lace. Collar: 4" x 21"; cuffs:
9¾" x 2¾"

Gift of Mrs. Charles O. Read. 25.006a–d

Lace using various colored yarns can be traced back to the early 17th century, when small edgings and insertions were made of braided linen threads. Heavy silk gimp and lace embroidered with details of fruits, flowers, and architectural scenes using colored silk threads became popular in the latter part of the century (cat. no. 54), but lost their popularity during the 18th century, when the emphasis changed to making lace as light as possible to resemble Indian muslin.

It was not until the mid-19th century that polychrome laces were again seen, when an interest developed in reviving earlier styles. Both France and England produced colored lace in centers like Le Puy, Caen, and Colyton in Devon. In 1874, Michelangelo Jeserum and the Countess Andriana Marcello established a bobbin lace industry in Pellestrina, near the mainland of Venice, specializing in polychrome laces. Mrs. Palliser describes the laces as "bobbin lace worked in colours with designs of flowers, fruits, leaves, arabesques, and animals, with the various tints and shading required."[1] Santina Levey describes an example of polychrome lace in the Victoria and Albert Museum, possibly from the workshop of Jeserum, as "fairly coarsely worked with a floral design of round flower-heads within a mesh of elongated leaves; it is made with bright green, red, yellow, and violet cottons."[2] Because both descriptions can be applied to the Museum's collar and cuffs, they have been attributed to the workshops of Pellestrina. The floral design of the collar and cuffs is similar to designs from the early part of the 20th century made in the lacemaking school on the island of Burano, also near Venice, suggesting that an early 20th century date is correct for these pieces.
P.P.

1. Palliser, *History of Lace*, pp. 62–63.
2. Levey, *Lace*, p. 112.

Color plate, page 35

85

M.L. Schwarz
Hungarian, Budapest

SZUR, early 20th century
Wool; felt, embroidered and appliquéd.
Center back length: 60"

Gift of Mrs. Wheelock from the Estate
of Miss Bertha Stevens. 1986.063

One of the most characteristic pieces of
Hungarian national dress is the szur. This
felted overcoat is a traditional garment
which has a long history among the Hungarian peoples. The garment is simply constructed, like most traditional Hungarian
dress, its pattern based on rectangles, or
loom widths. The coat, or cape, hangs
straight from the shoulders and has large
sleeves, into which the arms are never put.
In some szur coats the sleeves are closed at
the bottom and are used as pockets. A large
round collar extends down the front of the
coat in two large panels and is often the
site of elaborate embroidery.

Through time the szur became more and
more elaborate as it developed into a status
symbol. The coats were not made in the
home but were commissioned from local
szur makers; thus they were an expression
of wealth and can be identified as to provenance, since each region had a distinctive
variety of szur.

During the 20th century encouragement
by the government kept national dress an
important part of Hungarian life. As in
the past it was not only the peasants who
dressed themselves in this fashion, but
all classes, both urban and rural. The RISD
szur, made by a store in Budapest, M.L.
Schwarz, is a simplified example of
this traditional coat, made for an urban
clientele.

The very graphic design of the black-on-
white embroidery relates closely to the
patterns of the paper cut-outs that have
long been part of traditional folk art in
Eastern Europe.

P.P.

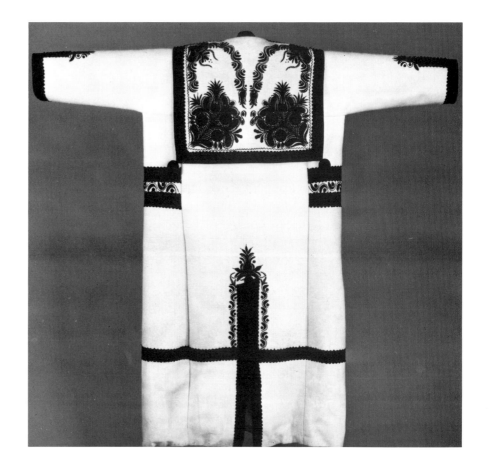

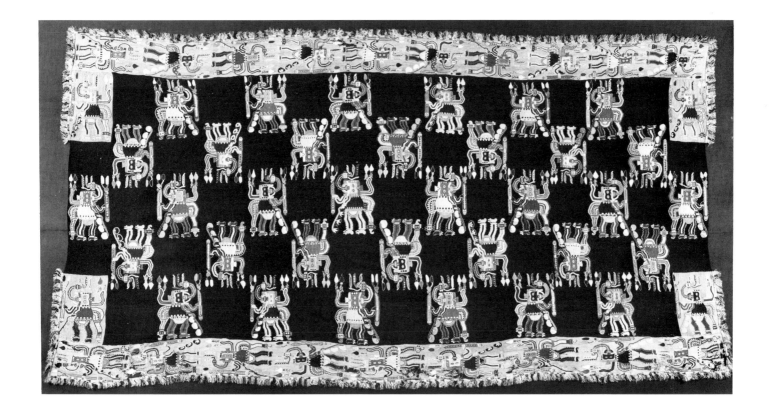

86

Peruvian, Paracas Peninsula, Early Intermediate Period, Epoch II, 300–200 B.C.

MANTLE
Alpaca wool, cotton; plain weave, embroidery. 50" x 93"

Museum Appropriation. 40.190

Publications: *Bulletin*, Dec., 1940, p. 80; Keleman, *Medieval American Art*, 2, pl. 177b; Kubler, *The Art and Architecture of Ancient America*, p. 148b; Willey, *Das Alte Amerika*, p. 326, pl. 42; *Handbook*, p. 297.

This textile probably originates from Cerro Colorado, a site on the Paracas Peninsula of the Peruvian coast. In this area, one of the most remarkable of the early Andean weaving traditions flourished around the first millennium B.C.

The preservation of fragile textiles like the RISD mantle and other highly perishable organic materials was due to burial in the desert of the southern Peruvian coast. Here a temperature inversion caused by a cold Pacific current next to the warm Peruvian coastal plain inhibits precipitation. Sizable communities had been established by at least 1500 B.C., their populations subsisting not on agriculture but on the extraordinarily abundant resources of the Pacific Ocean.

Of the many textiles found in Paracas funerary bundles, mantles such as RISD's are regarded as the most spectacular. The central panel of the RISD mantle is a plain weave made of very fine natural black alpaca wool. On this field, 34 anthropomorphic beings alternate in a checkerboard pattern. Narrow border panels with 23 figures embroidered end-to-end effectively frame the central panel. The background is filled with wool embroidery covering the foundation cloth with a veneer of subtle red color in knit stem stitch, a complicated technique that results in a tapestry-like effect. As a final finish, a short fringe manufactured separately was sewn to the edges of the border. Figures holding decapitated heads, depicted in the knit foundation section of this fringe, are an interesting detail representing trophies.

The 57 figures embroidered on the RISD mantle iconographically represent a single mythical being. Richly dressed in a tunic edged with representations of decapitated "trophy" heads and a skirt, this being wears a headband and mouth mask that are like gold ornaments made by ancient Peruvian goldsmiths. Also, it holds a staff with serpent or worm features and a string of beans, and has elaborate serpent-like appendages emerging from its mouth and trailing at its back. Stylistically the thumbed foot and grasping hand are important identifying features of Early Intermediate Period Epoch II designs.[1]

Since valuable products, including wool imported from the Andean highlands, cotton and dyes, as well as a great deal of expert human effort, went into the manufacture of fine cloth in ancient Peru, it was expressive of wealth and status and also considered an excellent ceremonial offering.

Like many of the finest Paracas textiles, this mantle was probably made solely as a mortuary offering to be buried with the dead and was never intended for use by the living. It is likely that this sacred function of cloth—as a sacrificial and burial offering, rather than as clothing for the living, its more prosaic function—led to the development of the Andean weaving tradition as one of the finest and most complex in the ancient world.

T.G.

1. Dwyer, "The Chronology and Iconography of Paracas-Style Textiles," p. 126.

Color plate, page 36

87

Peruvian, South Coast, late Nasca,
ca. 300 A.D.

BURIAL CLOTH
Wool; discontinuous warps and wefts.
64″ x 145″

Helen M. Danforth Fund. 79.153

Publication: *Museum Notes*, 1980, p. 9.

The Nasca culture of Peru (400 B.C.–500 A.D.) is best known for its rich polychrome ceramics, the giant figures and lines which cover the desert to the north of the Nasca valley, and the remarkably rich textile tradition demonstrated by burial offerings at Paracas, Ica and Nasca itself. This textile, almost certainly a burial offering, provides us with a unique insight into both the technical and aesthetic virtuosity of the Nasca weaver. It is relatively late in the Nasca stylistic sequence and was probably originally in one of the elite tombs at Nasca or in adjacent valleys such as Ica which were under Nasca control at the time.

Technically, it consists of two separately woven, four selvedge textiles sewn together. The construction of each section utilizes discontinuous warps and wefts in a complex manner which is peculiar to ancient Peru. Each block of color is a separate unit interlocking on all sides with neighboring color areas; this allows the formation of a design which is identified on both sides of the cloth, and yet the textile remains light and sheer. In order to produce this effect a system of supplementary scaffold yarns had to be constructed which would hold the warps in place and allow them to be interlocked. The wefts would have been inserted by the time-consuming process of needle weaving (similar to darning). Finally, the scaffolding would be removed from the finished textile. Apparently some of these scaffold yarns have been reused to join together the two sections of the RISD burial cloth.

Aesthetically, the great impact of the completed textile comes partly from the carefully controlled use of color and partly from the stylized and abstract figures which make up the overall design. The six repeated figures indicate what is apparently an important iconographic concern of the Nasca artist. They show the relationship between flying or floating mythical creatures and death, symbolized in this instance by trophy bodies. While geometricized because of the weaving technique, the figures can be read by reference to more representational versions painted on burial ceramics. In this case, the rear portion of the flying figure is viewed dorsally with splayed feet and bird tail. The head section faces us straight on, having eyes, nose and mouth clearly delineated below a stepped headdress with recurved elements suggesting feathers. Below the flying figure's head and grasped tightly in its arms is the head of a rectilinear trophy body. The art of the Nasca is filled with representations of head hunting, severed heads and trophy bodies. Caches of actual trophy heads, decorated for display, are often found in Nasca cemeteries. In many conventional Nasca representations, as in this one, the flying figure draws the trophy head or body to its mouth or touches it with its tongue. Perhaps this association has something to do with the burial ritual or with a more general belief in death and the afterworld. If this were so, it would be an appropriate scene for this elaborate textile offering. The tremendous investment of labor required to produce it shows that it had great value in ancient times. The complex iconography expressed in subtle color and refined design surely reflects the work of a great artist.

E. D.

88

Peruvian, Coastal Region, Huari, Middle Horizon, ca. 600–850 A.D.

TUNIC
Wool and cotton; tapestry weave. 43½" x 46½"

Mary B. Jackson Fund and Edgar S. Lownes Fund. 40.007

In the Middle Horizon (500–900 A.D.), the first two of the great highland empires were founded. Tiahuanaco state, based around Lake Titicaca, and the more northern state of the Huari, based around what is now the Peruvian city of Ayacucho, expanded westward, and dominated coastal areas with their political systems, religious beliefs, and commerce. Although the provenance of this tunic shirt is unknown, its fine state of preservation suggests that it was probably discovered on the coast, but the use of wool in the warp may indicate highland production.[1]

We have little information on how, and by whom, such a shirt would have been worn. Woven as two wide, but short lengths, it was seamed together at the center, leaving a hole for the head, then folded in half and seamed up the sides, leaving two holes for the arms. Worn this way, it would have hung about to the knees of an average sized man, and may have been worn with a loincloth underneath. Because of the extremely careful craftsmanship, the fine yarns, and good dyes, it was probably worn by a person of high status.

The techniques by which it was made point to a time-consuming process. Many interlocked threads (over 110 per inch) are built up in the tapestry technique completely covering the warp. Because it is so wide, it was very difficult for a single weaver to pass a single weft across the entire width of the fabric. In some areas, this problem was solved by the use of erratic and "lazy" wefts, which are built up small area by small area to make a wider block of solid color. It is also conceivable that several weavers, sitting side by side, worked simultaneously.

The iconography of Huari and Tiahuanaco weaving is characterized by highly abstracted symbols, unlike the detailed representation of men, animals and plants of earlier periods. The motifs on this shirt may represent an abstract feline head, with a round eye connected to a rectangular pendant shape, and a mouth represented by a letter-N shape indicating upper and lower fangs, a common motif in the art of the period.[2] Another stylistic feature common to the period is the presence of two pattern bands in each side: a wide one towards the center of the shirt, and a narrower one towards the side seams. The narrower band shows the same motifs as the wider one, but they are slightly compressed. Alan Sawyer suggests that more complex shirts with more drastic compression indicate a later period, so that this tunic would fall relatively early in the culture's history.[3]

A. W. F.

1. Bird and Skinner, "The Technical Features of a Middle Horizon Tapestry Shirt from Peru," p. 7.
2. Ibid., p. 11.
3. Sawyer, *Tiahuanaco Tapestry Design*, p. 8.

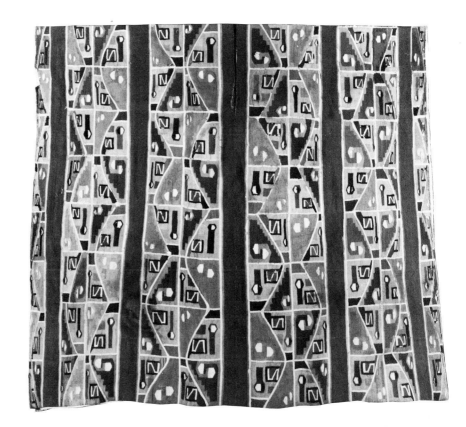

89

Peruvian, Central Coast, Chancay Valley,
Second Intermediate Period, 1100–1420

LOINCLOTH
Wool and cotton; plain weave alternating
with continuous warp patterning. 25½" x
15"

Museum Appropriation. 20.257

Between the time of the Tiahuanaco and
Huari empires and the time of the Inca
empire, the Second Intermediate Period
saw a group of separate and diverse states
and culture groups across the Central
Andean region. High standards of craftsmanship continued as the tapestry weaving
popularized by the Tiahuanaco and Huari

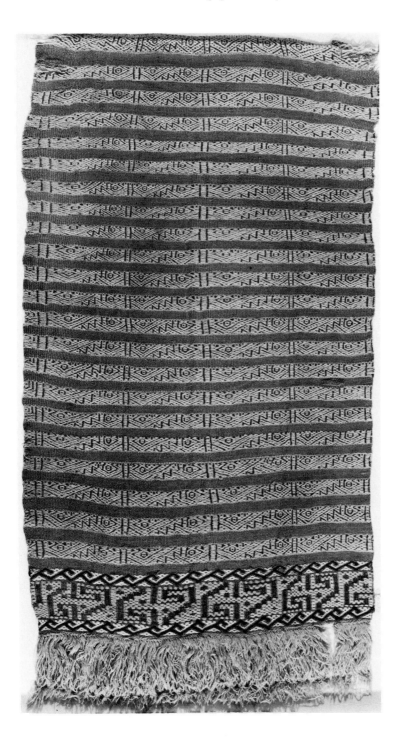

empires remained in great use, as did all
the techniques used in earlier periods.
More similarities are seen iconographically
across the region than in earlier periods,
suggesting that cloth was widely traded.[1]

Perhaps the largest and best known of
these states is the Chimu culture, whose
remains have been found on the north coast
of Peru. Although they never founded an
empire on the same scale as the Tiahuanaco/
Huari or the Inca, the Chimu expanded
into neighboring areas, influencing much
of the northern and central coastal regions
of Peru. From the archaeological remains
of their great city Chan Chan, as well as
several smaller ones, we know that the
Chimu had a well-developed urban society
complete with civic planning. The extensive building must have required a high
degree of organization, and subdivisions
and variation in housing indicate social
structures and class systems.[2]

The arts of the period tended towards
geometric patterning rather than the con-
crete representations of the Early Intermediate Period, or the elaborate abstractions of the Middle Horizon. Both the
quality and quantity of textiles produced
remained high, and many beautiful pieces
have survived.

Further to the south, several smaller
states occupied river valleys in the central
coast, and though influenced by Chimu
culture, they remained quite separate. The
state located in the Chancay valley was
one of these, and they also, as part of the
Cuismancu empire, had their own city-
state.[3] They were an urban society based
on agriculture, and are known for their
fine textiles and ceramics.

This woven loincloth from the Chancay
valley would probably have been worn
under a tunic or shirt of a shape similar to
the Huari tunic. It was woven with four
selvedges on a continuous warp loom out
of a combination of cotton and wool, and
uses both complementary and supplementary weft patterning to create rows of
geometric birds.
A. W. F.

1. Lanning, *Peru before the Incas*, p. 127.
2. Mason, *Ancient Civilizations of Peru*,
   p. 102.
3. Ibid., p. 104.

90

Peruvian, Coastal Region, Pre-Columbian

HEADDRESS
Wool and human hair; knotting and braiding. 35″ x 8″

Museum Works of Art Fund. 43.031

In some mummy bundles from the coast of Peru, a face mask was placed on the outside of the wrappings. In others, hats or headdresses were placed on the body. Some of the headdresses were made of camelid wool, while others, like this one, were made of human hair braided into many tiny braids. We may infer that this was a popular hairstyle of the day, and in fact in some regions of modern Peru and Bolivia, men and women still dress their hair in similar fashion.

This cap was made by braiding human hair onto a knotted skull cap of natural tan and brown shades of alpaca. The ends of the braids were decorated by colorful wrappings of fine wool yarn. Raoul D'Harcourt illustrates several similar caps in the collections of the Museum für Volkskunde in Berlin, the Göteborgs Museum in Sweden, and the Musée de l'Homme in Paris. The Paris cap, found on the central coast of Peru, is constructed in a manner similar to the headdress, but is covered with tufts instead of braids of human hair.[1]
A. W. F.

1. D'Harcourt, *Textiles of Ancient Peru*, pl. 78a,b,c.

91

Peruvian, Highland region, Inca,
1300–1500

TUNIC WAISTBAND
Wool and cotton; interlocked tapestry.
29¾" x 4¾"

Anonymous Gift. 52.353

In the 15th century, the Inca state grew
from a small highland community to
become one of the largest empires in history. Although it existed for less than a
century, the empire eventually stretched
from Central Ecuador well down into
Chile, covering a vast amount of territory.
The Incas did not just conquer and demand
tribute, but enforced their language,
religion, and social organization on the
people they conquered. In this organization cloth played a vital role.

John Murra discusses this point in depth,
explaining that cloth was one of "two main
economic obligations which the citizen had
toward the state." These obligations were
"to work the crown and churchlands . . .

(and) to weave cloth for crown and church
needs" and in return the citizen was guar-
anteed the "right to continue to plant and
harvest one's own crops on ayllu lands (and
the) right to wool or cotton from community stocks for the making of one's own
clothes."[1]

The decoration of cloth itself was important as a mark of class and social status.
There were laws about who could wear
what clothing: cloth made of vicuña fiber
was restricted to the use of the Inca and
those on whom he had bestowed the right
to wear it. Violations of this law were
punishable by death. Several chroniclers
reported cloth to be as important as llamas
or food as a religious sacrifice and it held
significance as part of proper burial.
Finally, cloth was an important gift. Murra
says that "exchanges of cloth were an
integral part of diplomatic and military
negotiations" and that a "textile 'gift'
[served at] the issuing of Inca citizenship
papers as a coercive and yet symbolic reit-
eration of the peasant's obligation to the
state, of his conquered status."[2]

Each family made fabric for household
use as well as garments for the state as tax.
Garcilaso de la Vega reported that women
usually wove "awasqua," for the lower
classes, while men were responsible for
"kumpi" cloth for the upper classes. But
not all the cloth produced for the states was
woven by peasant households. The
maidens of the sun, or "mamacunas,"
were cloistered women the Inca could take
or grant as wives. Their main task was to
weave and spin and they produced a large
quantity of cloth, especially the finest fabrics for the Inca's personal use, or for royal
gifts. Since the Inca is reported never to
have worn the same garment twice, his
personal attire must have accounted for
much weaving.[3]

Inca tunics were woven on wide but
short looms, folded in half, seamed up the
sides leaving armholes, and worn with the
warp horizontally.

This small piece is a fine example of the
kumpi tapestry cloth worn by men of the
nobility. This piece was the band of decoration found at waist level on many tunics,
woven separately and stitched on. Various
patterns have been described by Ann
Pollard Rowe, many of which involve
diamond and geometric patterns within
grids, but this does not seem to fit within
any of her named categories.[4]

A. W. F.

detail

1. Murra, "Cloth and its Functions in the Inca
   State," pp. 711–715.
2. Ibid., pp. 714, 721–722.
3. Garcilaso de la Vega, *Commentarios Reales
   de los Incas*, 1, pp. 8; 234–235.
4. Rowe, "Technical Features of Inca Tapestry
   Tunics," pp. 6–7.

92

Peruvian, Highland Region, Colonial
Period, 16th century

PANEL
Wool and cotton; interlocked tapestry.
47½" x 19"

Bequest of Martha B. Lisle. 67.435

After the Spanish conquest of the Inca
empire, the elaborate state system of
tapestry-cloth production was destroyed.
Today, most Andean cloth is warp patterned
and very few areas produce any tapestry,
although it was the glory of Inca weaving.
John Rowe suggests that the reason for this
was that tapestry was an art based on the
existence of a nobility which the Spaniards
eradicated.[1] George Kubler also notes that
the Spaniards both consciously and sub-
consciously caused the extinction of pre-
Columbian motifs as a way of asserting
and maintaining their position.[2]

But for a while, the Spaniards did try to
make use of the Andean's great skill in
weaving tapestry, and this small piece is an
example of a tapestry commissioned by the
Spanish but woven by Andeans.

As many of the chroniclers note, Europeans were highly impressed by Andean
weaving, and by 1565, colonial factories
were authorized to produce cloth for
the use of the Spaniards, primarily in
America.[3] Workshops sprang up all over
the Andes; anyone who could afford to
employed at least one weaver to produce
tapestries for his home or for sale. By
1584, Spain was reporting losses because
the "wine and woolen industries in Peru"
were producing so much that Spanish
merchants could not compete, and in 1612,
Philip II passed the Law of the Indies which
forbade competition with peninsular
merchants or trade between colonies.
Although illegal, tapestry production did
continue through the colonial period, and
in pieces such as this one, we can see the
combination of ideas, images, and techniques from the Andes and from Europe.

This piece is woven in an interlocked
tapestry technique identical to that used in
Inca pieces. For ease in weaving, a cotton
warp with a wool weft was used. The weft
is of brightly colored alpaca wool with
some silver-wrapped threads for special
details. The four-selvedge technique also
points to an Andean heritage.

The images show a combination of influences. Women in Andean dress accompany
a man in Spanish dress who plays a guitar.

Other images include plants, animals, fish,
baskets of fruit, and abstract designs similar to those used in Inca and Tiahuanaco
tapestries. Zimmern suggests that the edge
pattern was copied from floral designs on
Spanish lace and drawn work, but with the
addition of many Andean birds.
A. W. F.

1. Rowe, "Standardization in Inca Tapestry
   Tunics," p. 242.
2. Kubler, "On the Colonial Extinction of the
   Motifs of Pre-Columbian Art," pp. 14–34.
3. Zimmern, "The Tapestries of Colonial Peru,"
   p. 31.

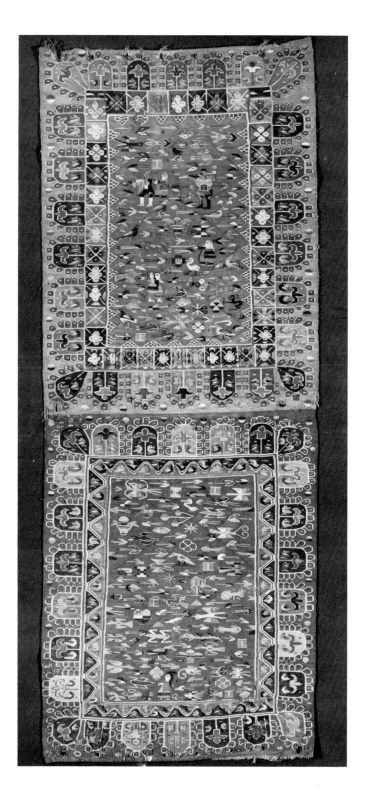

93

Bolivian, Macha, Provincia Chayanta,
Department of Potosí, mid-20th century

LLICLLA (carrying cloth)
Wool and cotton; warp faced plain weave,
supplementary patterning warps. 36″ x
41″

Gift of Mr. and Mrs. Peter Farago. 79.015

As in Pre-Columbian Peru, Andean weavers continue to create beautiful cloth, which not only is made by sophisticated techniques, but which also contains complex ideas and serves many uses. The north of the Department of Potosí, in Bolivia, is a remote, mountainous region in which Quechua and Akymara speakers live as self-sufficient farmers and herders much as their ancestors did hundreds of years ago, before the Spanish conquest. Women weave traditional four-selvedge Andean cloths for themselves and their families on staked-out, continuous warp looms. Men use European treadle looms brought by the Spanish to weave yardage for cut-and-tailored dresses, trousers and jackets.

This lliclla (carrying cloth) is a good example of the kind of weaving produced today in Macha, an "ayllu" or social unit, formed by geographic and genealogical rules, which includes the town of the same name as well as many smaller communities in the region. The function, materials, shape, and method of making this piece are typical of most contemporary ethnographic Andean textiles, and the specific colors, proportions, patterns, and techniques are typical of weavings from Macha.

Although the weave structures are very complex, the loom itself is fairly simple (made of several sticks and some strings), and cloths like this one are the products of many hours of labor. Although weavers in Macha use a number of string heddles, most of the complementary warp structures are created by hand-picking threads. A single weft row can take half an hour to complete.

Weaving progresses from one end; then the weaver turns the loom and works from the other end. The final wefts are difficult to insert since there is little warp slack left, and in this area, the terminal zone, the weaver drops any pattern. Andeans consider a neat terminal zone to be the sign of an expert weaver, and so the weaver of this piece must have been proficient. The entire

process is repeated for the second half of the lliclla, the two pieces are sewn together with a decorative embroidery stitch, and sometimes (though not on this piece), a decorative edge binding is added.

The entire cloth is symmetrical around a point in the center. The complementary weave structures create a cloth with two opposite faces, symmetrical back to front. The mirror halves are seamed together with the terminal zones aligned on opposite ends, creating a diagonal symmetry.[1]
A. W. F.

1. Cason and Cahlander, *The Art of Bolivian Highland Weaving*, Rowe, *Warp Patterned Weaves of the Andes*, Cassandra Torrico, personal communication, 1987, and the author's own observations in the Macha area were the sources for this entry.

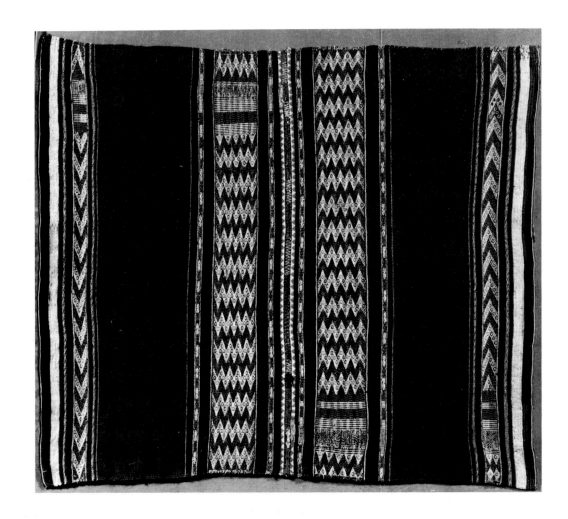

94

Mexican, first quarter of the 19th century

SALTILLO SERAPE
Wool and cotton; slit tapestry. 89″ x 51″

Gift of Mrs. Gustav Radeke. 16.002

"Saltillo" is the term given to a group of serapes which were made in northern Mexico during the 18th and 19th centuries. Saltillo was once one of the most important centers for their production, and a large trade fair was held yearly in the town, where the serapes were a much sought after item. But Saltillo was not the only center of manufacture. Documents show that the serapes were also woven in other northern Mexican towns: San Miguel de Allende, Guanajuato, Queretaro, San Luis Potosí, and Zacatecas.[1] The serapes are characterized by their beautiful and numerous colors which through the technique of slit tapestry form small, elaborate geometric patterns. All the serapes show three distinct fields: border, central medallion, and ground.[2] Although these serapes were extremely valued at the time of their manufacture and were eagerly collected, little documentation exists to establish the history of their development.

Archaeological finds from northern Mexico have shed some light on the serapes. Textiles, made of cotton dyed with indigo, found in dry caves in the state of Chihuahua, show patterns similar to the Saltillo designs with serrated concentric diamonds. Other textiles excavated in La Candelaria, 150 miles north of Saltillo, dating from 1000–1600, have related patterns. These finds show that the patterns of the Saltillo serapes existed in the area prior to the development of the serape but do not fully explain the development of the technique of tapestry weaving on a horizontal loom.

For this technique scholars point to the influence of the Tlaxcalans, one of the first peoples conquered by the Spanish in 1518. The Tlaxcalans were subjects of the Aztecs before the Spanish invasion, but quickly switched their allegiance to the Europeans. Throughout the Spanish colonization of Mexico the Tlaxcalans played an important role, especially in the north, where Tlaxcalan families were sent to provide an example to the recalcitrant northern peoples. With them they brought their customs and their crafts, including weaving in the European manner on horizontal looms, a method introduced to them by the Spanish, who wanted to develop the wool weaving industry in Mexico. It has been suggested that these Tlaxcalans, living in northern Mexico, developed the Saltillo serape using the horizontal looms of the Spanish and adopting designs from the people of the north.[3]

The serapes were an extremely well developed art form by the 18th century, to which the earliest surviving examples date. The classic phase of the Saltillo serape begins in the 18th century and lasts until the last quarter of the 19th. The Museum's serape dates from the first quarter of the 19th century when spotted light grounds, which contrast sharply with the serrated medallions in the center and the borders, were woven.

P.P.

1. Jeter and Juelke, *Saltillo Serape*, p. 11.
2. For a full discussion of the various types of Saltillo serapes see Brandford, "The Old Saltillo Sarape," pp. 271–292.
3. Jeter and Juelke, p. 13.

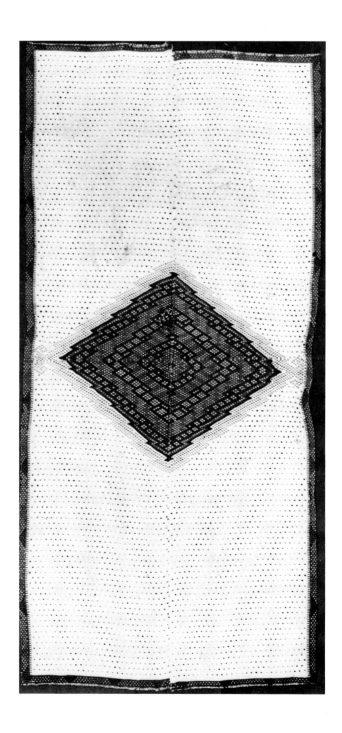

95

Navajo
North American

BLANKET, ca. 1860–1870
Wool; interlocked tapestry. 65¾" x 51¼"

Gift of Mrs. Murray S. Danforth. 45.081

When the Spanish arrived in the South-west they greatly changed the lives of the Indians, bringing with them sheep and horses, which the Navajo soon began to acquire through raids. The Indians gradually began to give up their nomadic existence to tend their growing flocks and herds. When the Pueblo Indians, in exile from the invading Spanish, began to settle with the Navajo, they introduced the technique of weaving on an upright loom.

The earliest extant examples of Navajo weaving were found in Massacre Cave in Arizona, where the Spaniards killed a group of Navajo in 1804. These fragments show the craft of weaving well developed by the early 19th century. By this time the Navajos were weaving horizontally striped blankets alternating natural white wools with brown natural yarns and indigo blue. One variation of this design, adapted from the Spanish sometime before 1800, was called "Moki" by the Navajo. In this design narrow stripes of blue and brown alternate with wider stripes of white.[1] The Museum's blanket is a variation of this design, showing later characteristics of Navajo blankets typical of the 1860s and 1870s: alternating stripes, zig-zags, and diamonds. The Navajo probably adopted these patterns from the basket weavers of their tribe whose coiled baskets are decorated with terraced and stepped triangles.[2]

By the mid-19th century the Navajo had added the color red to their textiles by weaving with red bayeta yarns. They had no easy way of achieving red by dyeing so they would unravel the Spanish baize, or bayeta, respin the threads and use them in their weaving. The stepped zig-zags of the Museum's blanket are woven with bayeta yarns S-spun with 3 to 5 strands. Bayeta yarns continued to be used into the 1860s when the Indians began to replace them with yarns from picked American wool flannel and later by aniline dyed yarns available through the traders.

P.P.

1. Wheat, "Documentary Basis for Material Changes and Design Styles in Navajo Blanket Weaving," p. 430.
2. Rodee, *Southwestern Weaving*, p. 2.

Color plate, page 37

96

Micmac
North American, Maritime Provinces

WOMAN'S HOOD, ca. 1775
Wool, silk ribbon, and glass beads; twill
weave, embroidered. 14½" x 8½"

Gift of Edward B. Goodnow. 81.019.10

"The Indian women here wear a short body-gown, and pointed conic headdress...;
and some of the cloth headdresses were beautifully worked in figures and tracery, with the moosehair and porcupine quills, dyed in bright colours," wrote Richard Bonnycastle of Micmac women in 1841.[1] Inhabiting the Maritime Provinces, the Micmac were among the first tribes to be subject to European contact, as early as the beginning of the 17th century. With French nuns came Venetian glass beads, easily applied to tradecloth garments, which began to take the place of skin garments and birchbark accessories decorated with quillwork.

By the 18th century, a second flowering of Micmac decorative art was occurring, as beautiful collars, moccasins, men's coats, and traditional women's conic hoods were decorated with fine beadwork. The RISD hood, on red tradecloth or "scarlet cloth," dates from the height of this new age of beadwork.

The "double-curve" motifs which decorate the hood are typical of Micmac decorative design and seem to be derived from ancient Micmac art before the time of contact with Europeans. Similar double-curve motifs occur in petroglyphs cut into rocks around Kejumkujik Lake, Nova Scotia. Rand's Micmac-English Dictionary lists a Micmac word "aboodlooagul," meaning just such "curious curves or flowers," and scholars have speculated that the motif derives from the medicinal herbs that were regarded by the Micmacs as protective and curative.[2] Speck, however, mentioned that nothing definite in the way of interpretation or symbolism could be discovered during his study of the motif in 1914, even after repeated inquiry.[3]

The Venetian glass beads on the RISD hood have been applied by stringing the beads on black horsehair, then couching the horsehair to the cloth, because the hole in the center of the beads was too small to accommodate a needle. Its red color is unusual, since most Micmac hoods seem to have been made of black cloth.
S.A.H.

1. Whitehead, *Micmac Quillwork*, p. 46, the main source for this entry.
2. Ibid., pp. 162, 164.
3. Frank G. Speck, "The Double Curve Motif in Northeastern Algonkian Art," Canada, Department of Mines Geological Survey, Memoir no. 42, Anthropological Series no. 1, 1914, reprinted in *Native North American Art History*, edited by Zena Pearlstone Mathews and Aldona Jonaitis, Palo Alto, California, Peak Publications, 1982, p. 387.

97

Athabascan, Tanaina
North American, Yukon Territory

SHOT POUCH, 1880–1900
Wool, cotton, beads, and leather; felt,
embroidered. 28" x 6¾"

Museum Works of Art Fund. 43.120

One of the results of European contact
with Native Americans was the introduction into the native design vocabulary of
floral beadwork motifs, a consequence of
European education brought by French
nuns. Establishing themselves first in
Quebec in the early 17th century, the nuns
moved westward with missionaries who
followed French traders and explorers,
founding mission schools in the midwest-
ern regions in the 18th century, and in the
western subarctic in the 1860s. Regarding
the skill of embroidery as a part of the
education of every proper young woman,
just as it was in Europe, the nuns made it
a regular part of the curriculum, teaching
both silk embroidery and the making of
beadwork, also popular at the time in
Europe. Evidence suggests that floral
patterns were drawn by the nuns and copied
by students, but the forms were adapted
by individual women to suit their own
preferences. In far eastern Canada, for
example, Micmac women subordinated
floral pattern to their own pre-contact
double-curve motifs (cat. no. 96). Realistic
European-style floral motifs were strongest
in the decorative arts of the Great Lakes
Ojibwa and Cree, but became more and
more stylized and simplified as this style of
decoration proceeded westward.

This shot pouch was made in the far
western region of the Yukon territory
between about 1880 and 1900, and shows
the result of this stylization of floral forms.
The flowers are reduced to arrow-like or
three or four petaled abstractions, on wide
and bulky stems with "hairs" or "thorns,"
a characteristic of far western flower
forms. Wholly unrealistically colored, the
flowers grow from "roots" that resemble
in no realistic way the roots of plants, but
suggest the roots of plants in herbals from
which the forms may have been taken by
the nuns centuries before. The double out-
lining and the metal points on the flowers
are also part of the far western vocabulary.

The shot pouch itself was a common
form among northern tribes, but was probably not worn while hunting. As the pris-
tine condition of this pouch suggests,
many were made for gifts, perhaps to
chiefs or for factors at the Hudson's Bay
Company. They were part of a man's
"dress up" attire worn for special occasions.[1]

S.A.H.

1. I am grateful to Barbara Hail, Haffenreffer
   Museum of Anthropology, Brown University, for much of the information contained
   in this entry.

98

Naskapi
North American, Labrador

HUNTER'S SHIRT, 19th century
Caribou skin; stamped with pigment.
38½" x 25½"

Museum Works of Art Fund. 44.593

Provenance: Heye Foundation

A nomadic tribe of hunters and fishermen, the Naskapi Indians of Northeastern Canada inhabited the Labrador Peninsula, an open plateau covered with grasses and lichen, the natural feeding ground for the herds of caribou which provided a mainstay for the Indians. Caribou meat was widely consumed and the skins and fur of the caribou were protection against the harsh climate of northern Canada. Because of the climate the Naskapi adopted the tailored shirt of the coastal Eskimos. In the winter the fur was left on the skin when the shirts were made and during the summer months the hair was removed from the skins.[1]

These caribou skin shirts were worn by men only when hunting, and it is possible that the designs which decorate them had some magical significance. The women of the tribes tailored the shirt to each man's body. The Museum's sizable coat was obviously made for a large, well-fed hunter. Most of the shirts are made in the same manner with a one-piece back with a triangular gusset at the lower back to allow more freedom of movement, a two-piece front, and sleeves. The Museum's shirt varies in that two gussets have been added at the center front to allow for the very full stomach of the wearer.

The shirt is decorated with red, blue, and yellow pigments which have been applied with a tool, similar to a stamp, which is dipped in the pigment and drawn across the skin. Before application the pigments were suspended in a combination of fish roe and water. The yellow color is the natural color of the fish roe, and the red and blue were achieved through the use of commercial pigments.

P. P.

1. Douglas, "A Naskapi Painted Skin Shirt," and Turner, "Ethnology of the Ungava District," were sources for this entry.

99

Sisseton Dakota
North American, South Dakota

DRESS, late 19th/early 20th century
Wool; plain weave; ribbon, sequin and
shell appliqué. 52½" x 61"

Museum Works of Art Fund. 44.592

Provenance: Heye Foundation

Often erroneously called "Sioux," the
Dakota tribes, together with the Lakota,
the Cheyenne, and the Arapaho, occupied
much of the Northern Great Plains from
the 18th century to the beginnings of the
reservation system in the 1860s and 70s.
Sharing linguistic similarities and the
nomadic life of the game hunter, these
tribes also shared certain cultural similarities, in particular, styles of decoration
and dress.

The basic prototype of women's dresses
in these tribes throughout the period was
a garment made out of two soft animal
skins, either elk or deer, seamed at the
sides with a hole at the top for the head.
The "legs" of the deerskin fell naturally at
the side edges of the skirt, creating interesting flags which were often decorated
with Venetian glass beads or dentalium
shells which matched or complemented
simple horizontal bands of beadwork on
the bodice of the dress.

When the heavy English woolen cloth
called Stroud (from its origin in Stroud,
England) began to be used as trade cloth
among the Plains tribes, women began to
make dresses of this material, keeping the
original skin pattern, complete with "legs"
at the side edges of the skirt.

This dress, although it is made from
many pieces of indigo-dyed Stroud, retains
the traditional shape as if it had been made
out of skins. The undyed white edges of

the cloth serve as decoration for the sleeve
and hem edges, and the dress is ornamented
with "precious tusk shells" in a circular
yoke at the neck. From the mollusc
Dentalium pretiosum, these shells are
native to Puget Sound, and were traded via
established networks to the Plains Indians.
Pink and orange silk ribbons further decorate the dress.

Collected on the Sisseton Reservation
in South Dakota, this dress is similar to
other examples in the Denver Art Museum
and the Museum of the American Indian,
Heye Foundation. It probably dates to
around the turn of the century.
S.A.H.

American, 18th or 19th century

DUMMY BOARDS
Wood, wool, cotton; embroidered, satin stitch, stem stitch. Man (57.199.1): 42″ x 15¾″; woman (57.199.2): 41¾″ x 14½″

Anonymous Gift. 57.199.1 and .2

Dummy boards are among the more elusive of decorative objects. Although they date only to the 17th century, historians have been baffled about their exact function. Other appellations for the tall wooden figures, "silent companions," "pictureboard figures," "companions of loneliness," "hospitality figures," or in French simply "poupée" (doll), suggest their varying function as ornaments in interior decoration.

Made of different soft woods, up to seven feet tall, and with either an attached wooden stand or a device at the back to permit hanging on a wall, only a small number of American figures survived in 1981, when an exhibition of dummy boards was held at the Rye Historical Society, New York, including figures of Benjamin Franklin and George Washington. A figure of Maria Tripp copied from Rembrandt's portrait survives in several versions, and indeed the origin of dummy boards has been traced to Holland, where the 17th century painter Cornelis Bisschop is supposed to have painted the first one.[1]

Ralph Edwards, in his *Dictionary of English Furniture*, gives several examples of dummy boards in use in Europe: in the Castle of Schaumberg dummy boards were placed around the dining room walls to make the room look full of guests, and in several English houses he places them at the tops of stairways or at the end of long hallways. A 17th century Dutch print shows a dummy board in use as an ornamental figure in a tavern. Their most essential feature, thus, was their "trompe l'oeil" quality.

All these dummy boards had likenesses either painted directly onto wood, or onto paper pasted onto a wooden stand. RISD's dummy boards appear to be unique because they are embroidered figures, sewn to a fustian lining and stuffed, then tacked and nailed to a stand made of yellow poplar, the latter identifying them as American since *Liriodendron tulipfera* does not grow anywhere else.

The RISD figures have been thought to have been made in the late 17th century because of their costume, he with the lace ascot and blue mantle, sash, and star of the order of the Knights of the Garter, she with tiered skirt and bejeweled neckline, but the identification of the stand as American makes this very unlikely. Possibly the embroideries were made at an early date and remounted on American stands in the 18th or 19th century.
S. A. H.

1. Fendelman, *Silent Companions*, pp. 5ff.

101

Sarah Larkin
American, Richmond, Rhode Island

PETTICOAT, ca. 1760
Wool; quilted. 29¾″ x 98½ ″

Lownes Memorial Fund. 34.025

To help alleviate the cold of New England, colonial women wore quilted wool petticoats beneath their gowns. Since the most popular style of dress was an open robe which allowed one to see the petticoat underneath, these were often elaborately embroidered or quilted.

The Museum's piece belongs to a large group of wool petticoats with known provenance in southern Rhode Island and eastern Connecticut.[1] Most are made of wool calamanco, a heavily glazed worsted wool plain-weave cloth imported from England. Needleworkers seem to have preferred solid colored cloths for their quilted petticoats in bright colors: red, blue, yellow, and pink.

Petticoats perpetuated English traditions of needlework and iconography. Found on the RISD petticoat are a series of symbols, all relating to the English monarchy. Perhaps the most striking is the coat of arms with lion and unicorn quilted in the center front of the petticoat. These were the arms of the King of England and were used by George I, George II, and George III until 1801. Encircling the shield is the phrase "LION AND UNICORN A FIGHT FOR THE CROWN 1760," a reference to the unification of the English and Scottish kingdoms during the early 17th century under James I.

The second text quilted into the petticoat, "ROYAL STATE AND HAPPY PAIR" surmounts a wreath enclosing two confronting doves, a symbol of concord. George III became King in 1760 and was married the following year, providing suitable inspiration for a petticoat with such royalist associations.

Unlike the other petticoats in this group, this example is signed by its maker, Sarah Larkin, who quilted her name into the work (visible on the right side of the photograph below). She has been tentatively identified as either of two Sarah Larkins, a mother and daughter. The mother, formerly Sarah Kenyon, married Nicholas Larkin in 1740 and gave birth to a daughter, Sarah, in 1741. Nicholas Larkin was a captain in the Richmond, Rhode Island, militia between the years 1756 and 1757 and fought for the British in the French and Indian Wars.
P.P.

1. Another wool petticoat in the Museum's collection (25.001) is said to be from Portsmouth, Rhode Island; another from Norwich, Connecticut is published in *Antiques*, 3, no. 3, p. 117, March 1923; and another in the collection of Williamsburg (1952–19) made by Abigail Trowbridge of Connecticut features the same coat of arms as the Museum's petticoat. Baumgarten, *Eighteenth-Century Clothing at Williamsburg*, p. 24.

American, mid-18th century

CANVAS-WORK PICTURE
Linen; wool and silk tent stitch embroidery. 23¾" x 24½"

Gift of Mrs. Jesse H. Metcalf. 23.075

Publications: *Bulletin*, 1928, pp. 15–18; Cabot, "Engravings as Pattern Sources," pp. 476–479; *Handbook*, p. 287.

The Museum's canvas-work picture belongs to a group of related needlework objects of the mid-18th century all depicting fashionably dressed figures in a pastoral setting. These pieces are commonly referred to as the "fishing lady" pictures because of the repeated appearance of an elegantly dressed women fishing beside a brook, a common courting pastime during the 18th century.[1] Although in the over 60 such needlework pieces that are in existence she appears in only eleven, the name has come to refer to all of them.

Canvas-work pictures, or tapestry work as it was sometimes called, came into fashion in 17th century England when women began imitating in needlework tapestries imported from Flanders. Popular themes for these embroidered pictures during the 17th century were biblical and mythological, and they often depicted Adam and Eve in a garden filled with exotic flowers and beasts. The garden was carried over into 18th century embroidery, where it became a more sentimentalized pastoral scene, as in the RISD embroidery.

Inspiration for the design of English and American embroidered pictures from the mid-18th century is drawn from popular engravings of the period. The Museum's picture, like many of the others, is a composite of various sources. The couple at the card table is taken from a painting by Nicolas Lancret (1690–1743), later engraved by N. Larmessin. This scene is combined with one from Aesop's "The Tortoise and the Hare" and depictions of a

wide variety of animal and plant life taken from traditional pattern books. These motifs are combined with the others without regard to proportion and perspective, a common feature in the "fishing lady" pictures.

Most pictures seem to have originated in Boston where embroidery teachers like Mrs. Susannah Condy drew patterns for canvas work for both her students and the general public.
P.P.

1. Cabot, "The Fishing Lady and Boston Common," pp. 28–31.

103

Nabby Martin
American, 1775–1864

SAMPLER, 1786
Linen; silk and metallic thread embroidery. 15″ x 10¾″

Museum Appropriation. 17.361

Publications: Krueger, *New England Samplers to 1840*, pl. 44; Ring, *Let Virtue be a Guide to Thee*, pp. 113, 220; *Handbook*, p. 228.

The RISD Museum has a collection of about 40 samplers; among them are at least seven of the finest samplers ever stitched in America, made between 1786 and 1796 by Rhode Island girls at the Mary Balch school in Providence.

In the late 18th century, women's education consisted of a few years' training in reading, writing, arithmetic, and needlework, with music and dancing often included among the "accomplishments" required of a young lady. These "branches of learning" were taught to girls in small "dame" schools run by local women.

Mary Balch grew up and was educated in Newport, the leading city in Rhode Island before the Revolution.[1] Newport, however, never recovered from British occupation between 1777 and 1780, and like many families, the Balches moved to Providence, where Mary Balch and her mother Sarah opened a dame school sometime in the 1780s. Trained in needlework in Newport, Mary Balch embellished and refined the techniques of sampler making which she taught to the girls in her "Female Academy," as it was called, demanding complexity of design and organization, and perfection in stitching.

Many of the samples she designed for her students resembled Nabby Martin's work, organized around representations of important Rhode Island buildings and incorporating fashionably dressed people in addition to the typical verses, floral designs, and alphabets. Nabby Martin's sampler pictures two buildings; at the center is a building identified in other samplers as "The State House" but it is unclear whether this is in Newport or Providence. At the top of the sampler is the College Building at Brown University with a slogan "To Colleges and Schools ye Youths Repair. Improve each precious Moment while you're there." That students had some leeway in lettering their samplers is shown by the crowding of the last word, "there," at the end of the bottom line and even into some space remaining on the top line. Miss Martin, the daughter of a Providence wheelwright and member of the Rhode Island Assembly, was unusually talented; at age 11 she was asked by Miss Balch to cover completely the background of her sampler with stitches, to include more verses instead of an alphabet, and to use many more different types of stitches than Cynthia Burr, aged 16, or Loann Smith, aged 13, whose very similar samplers made in the same year, are also in the RISD collection. In their colorful style and beautiful if naive complexity, these Balch school samplers form a body of work with a recognizable regional style, the products of an unusually artistic and inspiring teacher. Few other such complicated and appealing pieces appear in the entire history of samplers, which died out with the advent of more liberal education for women in the mid-19th century.

S.A.H.

1. Betty Ring tells the story of Mary Balch and her students' samplers in detail in *Let Virtue be a Guide to Thee*.

Color plate, page 38

104

Attributed to James Alexander
American, born Ireland, 1770–1870

DOUBLE WEAVE COVERLET, 1828
Linen and wool; double cloth. 97" x 78"

Bequest of Mrs. Elizabeth C. Story. 15.110

This coverlet, one of the earliest patterned wool and linen coverlets to be woven in America, is attributed to James Alexander, an Ulster-Scot who emigrated to America in 1798, after seven years spent as a weaver in Belfast. His account book, in the New York State Historical Society in Cooperstown, reveals that he settled in Little Britain, New York, near Newburgh, and then combined weaving with farming. His products included "diaper and damask diaper of the completest European patterns from 1 to 2 ½ yds wide, Flowered Carpets, Carpet Coverlids, full breadth or half, . . . Counterpanes, . . . together with all kinds of fancy weaving, . . . all kinds of Float Coverlids, carpets, single and double, and all kinds of plain work such as linen or woolen."[1] Not an itinerant weaver, Alexander may have used a draw loom in his shop to produce these household linens, since the jacquard machine did not arrive in America until 1825 and was not in common use until the 1830s. Most of the materials for coverlets came from the customers themselves, who hand-spun the woolen and linen yarns. Alexander advertised that "any person wishing to leave their work shall have it attended to with punctuality and done in a workmanlike manner." For the weaving of a coverlet Alexander charged between $2.00 and $5.50, but eventually he accepted pork, corn, "flower," or "chees" among many other commodities in exchange. At 78" wide with no center seam this "Flowered Coverlid" woven for Carline Row in 1828 is an example of the "full breadth" weaving referred to by Alexander in his advertisement.

Several other coverlets of similar pattern are known, of different dates between 1816 and 1839. The Museum owns another one with a horizontal instead of vertical orientation of the corner letters, which read, as in Carline Row's coverlet, "Agriculture and Manufactures are the Foundation of our

Independence July 4." The other RISD coverlet, made for Ann Conklin, bears the date of 1832, and is made up of two loom widths sewn together at the center. Since these coverlets are double-woven with two sets of warps and wefts, joined by interchanging the two at intervals, the descriptions and patterns on one side of the coverlet are reversed on the other, and it is impossible to tell which side of the coverlet is the face or front.

S. A. H.

1. *Political Index*, Newburgh, N.Y., May 8, 1820, reprinted in Parslow, "James Alexander, Weaver," p. 347.

105

Abigail Dewing
American, probably Massachusetts

ALBUM QUILT, ca. 1860–1870
Cotton; appliquéd and quilted. 97″ x 80″

Helen M. Danforth Fund. 1987.005

The album quilt became popular in the mid-19th century, when it was common for women to keep "albums" of friendship in book form. The classical album quilt has squares of differing patterns, appliquéd and often signed by many different people, a kind of album in cloth. Sometimes the squares were actually made by different people, but in this case, they are the product of one woman's needle.

Constructed of lightweight cotton squares, appliquéd in shades of red, brown, green, and yellow, this quilt has a vivid graphic quality. Its motifs include geometric shapes and florals, and, in each corner a combination of the two. The cross at upper right may be a fraternal symbol, commonly used on quilts at mid-century.[1] The swag border of this quilt is a feature often seen on quilts made in Baltimore, the center of the album quilt tradition, where extraordinarily complex and beautiful quilts with stuffed appliqué and unusual materials were made. But the Baltimore style of quilt was also made in other areas of the country, particularly in Pennsylvania, where, as in this rare New England example, the design might be simplified for local taste. Although the rest of the quilt is hand-sewn, the tiny outer border has been sewn on by machine in a lockstitch, indicating that the quilt was made toward the end of the 19th century.

The quilt came with an attached tag giving the maker's name, and the story that it had come from Rhode Island, but no date. Abigail Dewing has not so far been identified, but the Dewing family were early settlers in Massachusetts, around Boston. It came from a house in Warwick, Rhode Island, and, according to the attached tag, it was owned by George Ames.

S.A.H.

1. Kolter, *Forget Me Not*, pp. 38–40.

106

Bigelow Carpet Co.
Clinton, Massachusetts

WILTON CARPET, ca. 1909
Wool on jute backing; jacquard, cut pile.
105" x 144"

Edgar J. Lownes Fund. 85.012

Publication: *Museum Notes*, 1986,
pp. 19–20.

Erastus B. Bigelow, born in 1814 in West Boylston, Massachusetts, invented the basic carpet-making machines in the 1840s. In 1843 he invented a machine for making ingrain or Scotch carpeting, the ubiquitous double-cloth carpet that covered household floors from Maine to Virginia. But his invention in 1848 of a machine driven by steam power, that could make the more expensive Brussels or Wilton carpeting, was the basis of his worldwide renown. This machine and its products were exhibited at the London Exposition of 1851 and immediately became a sensation. Bigelow established his carpet company using this machine in Clinton, Massachusetts, in 1852. In 1899 Bigelow and the Lowell Manufacturing Company, where his ingrain machine was used, merged to become the Bigelow Carpet Company, which made this rug.

All the carpet machines invented by Bigelow worked on the principle of the jacquard loom but each gave a different effect. Ingrain was a flat-woven carpet and Brussels carpet had a looped surface. Wilton, the most esteemed of the three, was made like Brussels except that the loops were cut, giving a thick velvety pile. It had 50 per cent more wool than Brussels and was therefore more expensive. In 1900, according to a list of company products, five different styles of rugs were produced, including "Ardebil Wilton" patterned after the famous Ardebil Oriental carpet, "Bagdad Brussels," "Arlington," "Electra" and "Bagdad Wilton."

This carpet falls into the last category, since the name is woven into the jute backing of the rug. The Bigelow Company explained in a 1909 catalogue how this came to be: "So many attempts to substitute other makes of goods for *Bigelow* goods have come to our notice, that for the protection of our customers as well as ourselves, hereafter Bagdad Wilton and Bagdad Brussels Rugs will be branded with the word 'Bagdad' woven in the back of the right-hand border breadth of each rug." The fierce competition between Bigelow and other companies demonstrates how popular rugs like this had become since wall-to-wall carpet had declined in favor in the 1890s. According to *Suburban Life* of

1907, the Wilton carpet was "the" rug for general use, partly because Wiltons could be made to look so much like real Oriental carpets for a much smaller price.

Yet the "Bagdad" pattern is not a copy of any antique textile. Rather it is reminiscent of the Arts and Crafts tradition embraced by William Morris in England in the last quarter of the 19th century. While Western carpets "should equal the Eastern ones as nearly as may be in material and durability," said Morris, they "should by no means imitate them in design, but show themselves obviously to be the outcome of modern and Western ideas."[1]

The designer of this rug followed Morris's advice. The stylized motifs in the field of the rug are not taken from an existing Oriental design but are adapted and Westernized, and are reminiscent of the large repeating patterns employed by Morris in his own carpets. The rug has a large border filled with stylized leaf forms and winding stems, like a Morris border, and the leaves in the small outer border are nearly identical to the leaves in many of Morris's printed textiles.
S. A. H.

1. Morris and Co., *The Hammersmith Carpets*, catalogue, October 1882.

detail

107

Elizabeth Hawes
American, 1902–1971

EVENING GOWN, 1937
Silk; charmeuse. Center back length: 57"

Gift of the Design Laboratory, The Brooklyn Museum. 61.095.7

American fashion designers lagged behind their Parisian counterparts by more than 50 years in establishing themselves as couturiers known by name. Although the distinction of being the earliest American couturière belongs to Jessie Franklin Turner, who began designing elegant tea gowns under her own name in 1923, Elizabeth Hawes was the second to impress her name on the American fashion public.[1]

Born in Ridgewood, New Jersey, and educated at Vassar College, she began her career as an apprentice in the design workrooms of Bergdorf Goodman. Later she worked in Paris for a somewhat shady house engaged in obtaining Paris designs for Americans to copy, exercising her journalistic talents all the while by sending articles to *The New Yorker* and to a Wilkes-Barre, Pa. newspaper. A stint in the workrooms of couturière Nicole Groult, Paul Poiret's eccentric and demanding sister, was the final straw for Hawes, who left Paris to return to New York, declaring in a famous book about her Paris experiences, *Fashion is Spinach!*

In 1928 she opened a custom fashion salon, Hawes-Harden, at 8 West 56th Street, which became Hawes, Inc. in 1930. In 1932, Elizabeth Hawes became a well-known name when she was "discovered" and publicized by Dorothy Shaver at Lord and Taylor, one of the first American stores to feature and promote American fashion design.

In 1940, displeased with American fabrics and workmanship, she turned away from fashion design altogether, becoming Women's Editor of the left-wing newspaper *PM*, and designing uniforms for Red Cross volunteers in the war effort. After the war ended in 1945, she became an organizer for the United Auto Workers, specializing in recruiting women. She agitated for an end to discrimination against women in magazine and newspaper articles and in a book, *Men Can Take It*, illustrated by James Thurber (1939).

In 1948 she returned to designing, opening a new shop in New York, but she retired to California after 1951.

This dress, one of two owned by the Museum, is quintessential 1930's Hawes, embodying her characteristic color combinations and a flowing bias cut influenced by the French designer Madeleine Vionnet. Hawes's elegant gowns required a perfect figure, since they were worn with little underneath. They were an early instance of the complete liberation of women's bodies from restrictive underclothing. Unconventional to the end, Hawes also promoted tailor-made clothing for women and was a pioneer in men's fashion, showing clothes she worked out with a tailor's advice. It is for dresses like this, however, that she is best known.
S.A.H.

1. The Museum's collection of eight examples of Turner's work is an important resource. See *Museum Notes*, 1987, p. 18.

Magda Polivanov
American, born Russia, 1909–1985

CAPE, ca. 1940
Cotton; block-printed. Center back
length: 44″

Gift of Pauline C. Metcalf and Esther E.M.
Mauran. 1987.090

Publication: *1900 to Now*, pp. 70, 129.

The daughter of the last Czar's Imperial
War Minister, Magda Polivanov escaped to
England during the Russian Revolution in
1917. Here she studied painting at the
Royal Academy and the Slade School,
eventually coming to the United States in
1934. In New York she began a hand-
blockprinting and clothing business in the
late 1930s. She specialized in hand-
blockprinted muslin which was sewn into
curtains, cushion covers, and informal
clothing, or what is now called resort wear.

From 1937 to 1939 her designs were featured in major fashion magazines and
newspapers, often modeled by society
women or starlets. Like the Museum's
coat, they were designed for a lifestyle of
leisure and beachgoing, and according to
Eleanor Roosevelt, who owned some of
Polivanov's summer outfits, they were
comfortable and practical.

Magda Polivanov was involved in every
stage of a garment's production. The
clothes were sewn together before being
printed because varying sizes required different placement of the print blocks. She
then oversaw every step of the printing,
from carving the blocks to preparing the
dyes to the actual printing of the piece.
She used large blocks of color, and simple
images that related to the use of the piece,
like the fish, octopus and waves on RISD's
beach coat.

In later years Polivanov spent much of
each winter in Providence, where she had
a studio on Planet Street, and was a familiar figure on the East Side.
P.P.

109

Charles James
American, born England, 1906–1978

BALLOON DRESS and accompanying form,
1955
Silk; velvet. Center back length: 55″

Gift of Mrs. William Randolph Hearst, Jr.
57.192a,b

Publication: Coleman, *The Genius of Charles James*, p. 128.

Born of an English father and an American mother, Charles James spent his life alternating between the United States and Europe. After completing his schooling in England he decided to settle in his mother's home town, Chicago, where he began a successful millinery business under the label "Boucheron." His hats presage his later gowns in their sculptural forms created by simple folds of fabric.[1] In 1929, when he moved to London, he set himself the task of learning the art of the couturier. He showed his first line in Paris in 1937, and, in 1945, with a small inheritance and support from Mrs. William H. Moore, he opened his own small salon on Madison Avenue in New York.

During James's years in the United States he isolated himself from yearly trends in fashion, working closely with a small but select clientele. Unlike the designers working on Seventh Avenue, he was not interested in developing new designs on a yearly basis, but in continually perfecting his work, and would even recall a gown already sold to a client to make some small change.

James is best remembered for his extravagant ball gowns originally designed for these select clients. Fortunately for him his clientele was extremely loyal, since without their financial support James could not have produced as long as he did. One of the most famous was Mrs. William Randolph Hearst, Jr., wife of the newspaper magnate, and donor of the Museum's blue velvet gown. James designed the Balloon Dress for Mrs. Hearst in 1955 to be worn to the January 1956 March of Dimes ball at the Waldorf Astoria Hotel. The ball was an annual event and the appearance of several James creations was eagerly awaited by those attending.

The gown is made of royal blue silk velvet purchased by Mrs. Hearst from Saks Fifth Avenue for $1200.[2] It is an exemplary piece of Charles James's work, and is comparable to a piece of soft sculpture, since inside it James created an elaborate understructure of buckram and tapes, making the gown totally self-supporting.
P. P.

1. A rare early example of a James hat under the label Boucheron of lavender balibuntal straw is also in the Museum's collection.
2. Coleman, p. 128.

Color plate, page 39

110

Claire McCardell
American, 1905–1958

DRESS, ca. 1950
Wool; plain weave. Center back length: 47″

Gift of Mrs. Warren E. Teixeira.
58.173.1 a,b

Claire McCardell grew up in Frederick, Maryland, was educated at Hood College and the New York School of Fine and Applied Arts (now Parsons School of Design), and spent a year in its branch in Paris. In 1929 she became an assistant to the designer Robert Turk, and moved with him to the firm of Townley in 1931. When he was killed in an accident in 1932, she took over his position, designing successfully for Townley until her death. In 1942 Dorothy Shaver began to promote American design at Lord and Taylor, featuring Claire McCardell in her advertising.

McCardell was perhaps the greatest of the early sportswear designers, refusing to design anything complicated or uncomfortable. Her forte was cotton clothing such as the "popover" dress, a runaway best-seller, which could be an apron one minute and a party dress the next. Her "monastic" dress of 1938 was a simple triangular jersey dress shaped only with a tied belt; and her full-skirted silhouette with small bodice dominated the 1950s.

In her book *What Shall I Wear?* she put into writing the philosophy which underlay her designs, which were so radically different from the tight, constricting, albeit chic clothes inspired by French couture. "Clothes are for real live women," she wrote. "Fashion [is] linked to the woman who wears the fashion. . . . She must dress for her life. Physical ease is important, and even more important, mental ease."[1] Her dictum, "above all be comfortable," was a declaration of independence for American women, who could no longer afford to be held back by their clothes in lives that included going out to work, driving cars, and engaging in sports.

This yellow and green plaid dress has a natural waistline, industrial hooks and eyes to close the front, pockets, and a witty attached scarf, all hallmarks of the best features of Claire McCardell's designs.
S.A.H.

1. McCardell, *What Shall I Wear?*, p. 1.

Dorothy Liebes
American, 1899–1971

TEXTILE SAMPLE, ca. 1950
Wood, Lurex, and chenille yarn; plain
weave. 9½" x 10¼"

Gift of the Textile Department, RISD.
83.021.26

Born in Santa Rosa, California, Dorothy
Liebes studied art at the University of
California at Berkeley and began to weave
during this period. After obtaining an
M.A. from Columbia University, she con-
tinued her education in 1920 at Hull
House in Chicago, where weaving was
taught at the famous settlement house.

She opened her first studio in San Francisco in 1930, producing hand-woven textiles for artists and decorators. But Liebes's
best known work dates from the 1940s and
50s, when she produced handweaving in
new materials, making window blinds, for
example, from strips of wood, branches, or
grasses combined with highly colored,
unusual yarns. Liebes employed spinners
to hand-produce novelty yarns that were
hand-dyed to her order, and the highly
unusual combinations she made with these
yarns, together with her use of the new
metallic yarns, cellophane, Lucite, and
leather strips often metallically finished,
became an influential style in interior
decoration. In 1948 she moved to New York,
where she turned to industrial production.
When she died in 1971, the studio distributed her archive of samples to schools
throughout the country; the collection
acquired this window shade sample in
1983, when the Textile Department of the
Rhode Island School of Design donated the
samples it had received to the Museum.
S.A.H.

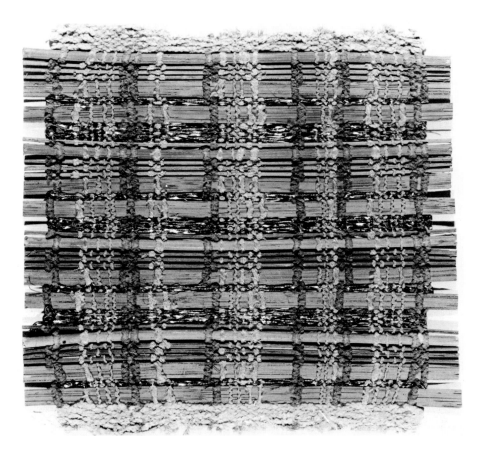

112

Cynthia Schira
American, born 1934

NIGHT GAMES, 1981
Cotton; jacquard. 18" x 14"

Gift of Cynthia Schira. 82.112

Publication: Marcoux, *Jacquard*, n.p.

Cynthia Schira graduated from the Rhode Island School of Design in 1956 and has since become a fiber artist of international repute. Prior to 1981 much of her work was produced in her studio on a hand loom, where she created woven pictures in which supplemental wefts were inserted by hand, making her woven pictures textural landscapes. "Night Games," in contrast, was woven at RISD on the jacquard loom used by the School of Design in its instruction. Although Schira was introduced to the jacquard loom through a textile design assignment while she was an undergraduate at RISD, it was not until 1981, when she and other prominent fiber artists were invited by RISD's Alice Marcoux to experiment with the loom and its possibilities, that she became fascinated with its freedom and restrictions.

Before the invention of the jacquard attachment in 1804 by Joseph Jacquard, figured textiles were woven on a drawloom which required two operators, a weaver and a drawboy. It was the job of the drawboy to pull a specific cord or leash to create a line of pattern or shed with the warp threads, into which the weaver could insert the weft threads, a very laborious and time-consuming process. The jacquard mechanism replaced the drawboy and automatically created the correct shed with a series of punched cards, a precursor of the modern computer. The mechanization of the drawboy's job saved much time and labor but also restricted the size of the pattern repeat. It was this dichotomy in the jacquard mechanism which so fascinated Schira in her work on the loom: how to maximize the ability to create complex weave structures on the loom because of its mechanization and how to minimize the restrictions on the repeat. In "Night Games," while restricted by a repeat 7½" x 4", she employed variation in weave and in the choice of weft thread to create a changing landscape on the surface of the textile.

During the RISD jacquard project the ease of weaving with a mechanical loom and the complexity of structure which can be achieved inspired Schira to think about her previous work. How could she continue to use the complexity of structure offered by the jacquard mechanism but still have the freedom of a hand-operated loom? This question took Schira to the Cooper Hewitt Museum in New York, where she studied complicated drawloom structures of the 18th century. In 1982 she won a Craftsman's Fellowship from the National Endowment for the Arts, which allowed her to purchase a computerized Macomber hand loom and to work for a year, which stretched into two, on the new loom. The computer replaces the jacquard cards on the Macomber, and allows her to experiment with complex structures but still retain the freedom to manipulate the threads by hand. Her work has now developed into complex triple weave canvases which allow the three layers of cloth to interweave with each other, creating various layers and textures within the structure of the piece and producing a very painterly cloth.
P.P.

Color plate, page 40

113

Red Grooms
American, born 1937
Lysiane Luong
American

MUMMY BAG, 1986
Cotton; hand screenprinted.
46″ x 23″ x 4″

Acquired through the generosity of
Norman J. Bolotow, Dr. and Mrs. Joseph
Chazan, Steven L. Lerner, Mrs. Frank
Mauran, Mr. and Mrs. Houghton P.
Metcalf, Jr., Mrs. and Mrs. Ernest Nathan,
and Roslyn H. Winograd. 1987.045

Painter, printmaker, moviemaker, holder
of Happenings, sculptor, Red Grooms is an
artist of great originality who in this work
has applied his prolific talent to textiles for
the first time. Born in 1937, he is part of
the generation that rejected Abstract
Expressionism, including Jim Dine, Alex
Katz, Claes Oldenburg, and others who
formulated Pop Art in the late 1950s and
early 60s. Grooms, however, is not strictly
a Pop artist and in fact specifically rejects
such a classification of his work, although

the similarity of approach is clear. Like
many Pop artists, Grooms has rejected
abstraction altogether and uses humor and
satire in hilarious and even vulgar ways to
point to the foibles of modern life and
modern society.

This good humor and gentle satire are
present in "Mummy Bag," a garment bag
which could actually be used as a piece of
luggage. It was designed and produced in
1987 by Grooms, Lysiane Luong, and a
team of assistants at the Fabric Workshop
in Philadelphia. The work, the only textile
object Grooms has designed, has an elaborately decorated coffin of an Egyptian king,
perhaps King Tut, on the front, but on the
back of the bag, Grooms has printed a view
of the mummy inside the coffin, wrapped
raggedly in linen strips and with blackened
toes protruding. King Tut, in spite of his
celebrity, is in reality just another mummy.
The satire extends to those modern yuppies
who carry garment bags on their jet-set
business trips and refers in its title to the
hippies of the 1960s who slept in sleeping
bags called mummy bags. On another level,
the work may even make fun of our pen-
chant for putting things inside things ad
infinitum–the mummy inside the coffin;
the dirty clothes in the traveler's garment
bag. The decoration of the bag has Grooms's

characteristic cartoonlike drawing, willful
distortion, exaggeration, and celebration
of the vulgar.

The Fabric Workshop in Philadelphia,
where "Mummy Bag" was printed, is
a cooperative workshop dedicated to
encouraging artists to produce hand screen-
printed textiles of all kinds. Founded in
1977 by Marion Stroud, Carolyn Ray, and
other artists and craftsmen, it brings artists
to its workrooms for a period of residence,
during which they learn the medium of
screenprinting and create designs for textiles that can then be produced by the
Workshop staff. Supported by grants from
the National Endowment for the Arts, the
Fabric Workshop has offered fellowships to
Joyce Kozloff, Philip Maberry, Brad Davis,
Roy Lichtenstein, and Robert Venturi,
among many others, in an effort to bring
about leaps of artistic creativity as these
artists apply themselves to the task of
learning what is for them a completely
new medium.
S.A.H.

Selected Bibliography

Abegg, Margaret. *Apropos Patterns*. Bern: Abegg-Stiftung, 1978.

Ackerman, Phyllis. *The Rockefeller McCormick Tapestries*. New York: Oxford University Press, 1932.

Ackerman, Phyllis. "Textiles of the Islamic Periods." In *A Survey of Persian Art*, edited by Arthur Upham Pope and Phyllis Ackerman. Oxford: Oxford University Press, 1938.

Adams, Marie Jeanne. *System and Meaning in East Sumba Textile Design*. Cultural Report Series no. 16. New Haven, Connecticut: Yale University Southeast Asia Studies, 1969.

Adams, Monni. "Kuba Embroidered Cloth." *African Art*, 22, no. 1 (1978), pp. 24–39; pp. 106–107.

Adams, Monni. *Designs for Living*. Cambridge, Massachusetts: Carpenter Center for the Visual Arts, Harvard University, 1982.

Aga-Oglu, Mehmet. *Safawid Rugs and Textiles*. New York: Columbia University Press, 1941.

Ames, Frank. *The Kashmir Shawl and its Indo-French Influence*. Woodbridge, Suffolk: Antique Collector's Club, Ltd., 1986.

Arwas, Victor. *The Liberty Style*. New York: Rizzoli, 1979.

Atil, Esin. *The Age of Sultan Süleyman the Magnificent*. Washington, D.C.: National Gallery of Art, 1987.

Baginski, Alisa, and Amalia Tidhar. *Textiles from Egypt 4th–13th Centuries C.E.*. Jerusalem: L.A. Mayer Memorial Institute for Islamic Art, 1980.

Baumgarten, Linda. *Eighteenth Century Clothing at Williamsburg*. Williamsburg, Virginia: Colonial Williamsburg Foundation, 1986.

Bennett, Anna Gray. *Fans in Fashion*. San Francisco: Fine Arts Museums of San Francisco, 1981.

Bennett, Anna Gray. *Unfolding Beauty: The Art of the Fan*. Boston: Museum of Fine Arts, 1988.

Bier, Carol, ed. *Woven from the Soul, Spun from the Heart: Textile Arts of Safavid and Qajar Iran, 16th–19th Centuries*. Washington, D.C.: Textile Museum, 1987.

Bird, Junius B., and Milena Dimitrijevic Skinner. "The Technical Features of a Middle Horizon Tapestry Shirt from Peru." *Textile Museum Journal*, 4, no. 1 (1974): pp. 5–13.

Brandford, Joanne Segal. "The Old Saltillo Sarape." In *Ethnographic Textiles of the Western Hemisphere. Irene Emery Roundtable on Museum Textiles, 1976 Proceedings*, edited by Irene Emery and Patricia Fiske. Washington, D.C.: Textile Museum, 1976.

Brédif, Josette. *Les Mouchoirs Illustrés de Rouen au XIXe siècle*. Jouy-en-Josas: Musée Oberkampf, 1986.

Bühler, Alfred. "Patola Influences in Southeast Asia." *Journal of Indian Textile History*, no. 4 (1959): pp. 4–46.

Bühler, Alfred, and Eberhard Fischer. *The Patola of Gujarat*. Basel: Krebs AG, 1979.

Bühler, Alfred, Urs Ramseyer, and Nicole Ramseyer-Gygi. *Patola und Geringsing*. Basel: Museum für Volkerkunde; Schweizerische Museum für Volkskunde, 1975.

Bulletin of the Museum of Art, Rhode Island School of Design. Providence, Rhode Island: Museum of Art, Rhode Island School of Design, 1913–1979.

Cabot, Nancy Graves. "The Fishing Lady and Boston Common." *Antiques*, 40, no. 1 (1941): pp. 28–31.

Cabot, Nancy Graves. "Engravings and Embroideries." *Antiques*, 40, no. 6 (1941): pp. 367–369.

Cabot, Nancy Graves. "Engravings as Pattern Sources." *Antiques*, 58, no. 6 (1950): pp. 476–481.

Cammann, Schuyler. *China's Dragon Robes*. New York: Ronald Press, 1952.

Canorella, Deborah. "Fabric About Fabric, Junichi Arai's Computer Creates a Textile for the 80s." *Threads*, no. 1, (1985): pp. 72–73.

Carlano, Marianne, and Larry Salmon, eds. *French Textiles From the Middle Ages Through the Second Empire*. Hartford, Connecticut: Wadsworth Atheneum, 1985.

Cason, Margorie, and Adele Cahlander. *The Art of Bolivian Highland Weaving*. New York: Watson Guptill, 1976.

Cavallo, Adolph S. *Tapestries of Europe and of Colonial Peru in the Museum of Fine Arts, Boston*. Boston: Museum of Fine Arts, 1967.

Chassagne, Serge. *Oberkampf, Un Entrepreneur Capitaliste au Siècle des Lumières*. Paris: Editions Aubier Montaigne, 1980.

CIETA. *Vocabulary of Technical Terms*. Lyon: Centre International d'Étude des Textiles Anciens, 1964.

Coleman, Elizabeth Ann. *The Genius of Charles James*. New York: Brooklyn Museum, 1982.

Davison, Mildred, and Christa C. Mayer-Thurman. *Coverlets*. Chicago: Art Institute of Chicago, 1973.

De Mott, Barbara. "The Spiral and the Checkerboard." In *African Art as Philosophy*, edited by Douglas Fraser. New York: Interbook, 1974.

De Osma, Guillermo. *Mariano Fortuny: His Life and Work*. New York: Rizzoli, 1980.

Deslandres, Yvonne. *Poiret*. Paris: Éditions du Regard, 1986.

D'Harcourt, Raoul. *Textiles of Ancient Peru and their Techniques*. Seattle: University of Washington Press, 1962.

Digby, George Whitfield. *Elizabethan Embroidery*. New York: Thomas Yoseloff, 1964.

Dimand, M S *A Handbook of Muhammadan Art*. New York: Hartsdale House, 1947.

Douglas, F.H. "A Naskapi Painted Skin Shirt." In *Material Culture Notes*. Denver: Denver Art Museum, 1969.

Dwyer, Jane Powell, and Edward Bridgman. *Traditional Art of Africa, Oceania, and the Americas*. San Francisco: The Fine Arts Museum of San Francisco, 1973.

Dwyer, Jane Powell. "The Chronology and Iconography of Paracas-Style Textiles." In *The Junius B. Bird Pre-Columbian Textile Conference*, edited by Ann Pollard Rowe. Washington, D.C.: Textile Museum, 1973.

Emery, Irene. *The Primary Structures of Fabrics, an Illustrated Classification*. Washington, D.C.: Textile Museum, 1980.

Fanelli, Rosalia Bonito. *Five Centuries of Italian Textiles: A Selection from the Museo del Tessuto, Prato*. Prato: Museo del Tessuto, 1981.

Fenaille, Maurice. *État général des Tapisseries de la Manufacture de Gobelins depuis son Origine jusqu'à nos Jours 1600–1900*. Paris: Imprimerie Nationale, 1904.

Fendelman, Helaine W. *Silent Companions*. Rye, New York: Rye Historical Society, 1981.

Fiske, Patricia L., W. Russell Pickering, and Ralph S. Yohe, eds., *From the Far West: Carpets and Textiles of Morocco*. Washington, D.C.: Textile Museum, 1980.

Floud, Peter. "English Printed Textiles VII. Prints of the 1820s." *Antiques*, 72, no. 5 (1957): pp. 456–459.

Garcilaso de la Vega. *Commentarios Reales de los Incas*. Buenos Aires: Emece Editores, 1943.

Gathercole, Peter, Adrienne L. Kaeppler, and Douglas Newton. *The Art of the Pacific Islands*. Washington, D.C.: National Gallery of Art, 1979.

Gilfoy, Peggy Stoltz. *Fabrics in Celebration from the Collection*. Indianapolis: Indianapolis Museum of Art, 1983.

Gittinger, Mattiebelle. *Master Dyers to the World*. Washington, D.C.: Textile Museum, 1982.

Greer, Louise, and Anthony Harold. *Flying Clothing*. Shrewsbury, England: Airlife Publishing, 1979.

Hayes, William C. *The Scepter of Egypt: A Background for the Study of Egyptian Antiquities in the Metropolitan Museum of Art, Part I: From the Earliest Times to the End of the Middle Kingdom*. New York: Metropolitan Museum of Art, 1953.

Hiroa, TeRangi. *Samoan Material Culture*. Bernice P. Bishop Museum Bulletin 75. Honolulu, 1930.

The Indian Heritage. Court Life and Arts under Mughal Rule. London: Victoria and Albert Museum, 1982.

Irwin, John. "Origins of the Oriental Style in English Decorative Art." *Burlington Magazine*, 97, no. 625 (1955): pp. 106–114.

Irwin, John, and Katharine B. Brett. *Origins of Chintz*. London: Her Majesty's Stationery Office, 1970.

Ishimura Hayao and Maruyama Nobuhiko. *Robes of Elegance*. Raleigh: North Carolina Museum of Art, 1988.

Jacqué, Jacqueline, and Véronique de Bruignac. *Toiles de Nantes des XVIIIe et XIXe Siècles*. Mulhouse: Musée de l'Impression sur Étoffes, 1977.

Jennes, Diamond. *Indians of Canada*. 7th ed. Toronto: University of Toronto Press, 1977.

Jeter, James, and Paula Marie Juelke. *The Saltillo Serape*. Santa Barbara: New World Arts, 1978.

Kahlenberg, Mary Hunt. *Rites of Passage*. La Jolla, California: Mingei International Museum of World Folk Art, 1979.

Katazome: Japanese Stencil and Print Dyeing: Tradition and Today. Tokyo: The National Museum of Modern Art, 1980.

Katzenberg, Dena S. *"And Eagles Sweep Across the Sky": Indian Textiles of the North American West*. Baltimore: The Baltimore Museum of Art, 1977.

Kaufman, Alice, and Christopher Selser. *The Navajo Weaving Tradition 1650 to the Present*. New York: E.P. Dutton, 1985.

Keleman, Pál. *Medieval American Art*. New York: Macmillan, 1946.

Kelsey Museum of Archaeology. *The Art of the Ancient Weaver*. Ann Arbor: The Kelsey Museum of Archaeology, University of Michigan, 1980.

Kendrick, A.F. *Catalogue of Textiles from Burying Grounds in Egypt*. London: Victoria and Albert Museum, 1920.

Kendrick, A.F. *English Needlework*. London: A. and C. Black Ltd., 1933.

King, Donald. *British Textile Design in the Victoria and Albert Museum*. Tokyo: Gakken, 1980.

Kolter, Jane. *Forget Me Not: A Gallery of Friendship and Album Quilts*. Pittstown, New Jersey: Main Street Press, 1985.

Kooijman, Simon. *Tapa in Polynesia*. Honolulu, Hawaii: Bishop Museum Press, 1972.

Krueger, Glee. *New England Samplers to 1840*. Sturbridge: Old Sturbridge Village, 1978.

Kubler, George. *The Art and Architecture of Ancient America*. Baltimore: Penguin Books, 1962.

Kubler, George. "On the Colonial Extinction of the Motifs of Pre-Columbian Art." In *Essays in Pre-Columbian Art and Archaeology*, edited by Samuel K. Lothrop. Cambridge, Massachusetts: Harvard University Press, 1961.

Kühnel, Ernst. *Islamische Stoffe aus Ägyptischen Gräbern*. Berlin: Staatliche Museen, 1927.

Kühnel, Ernst. *The Textile Museum: Catalogue of Dated Tiraz Fabrics, Umayyad, Abbasid, Fatimid*. Washington, D.C.: National Publishing Co., 1952.

Lamb, Venice. *West African Weaving*. London: Duckworth and Co., 1975.

Lanning, Edward P. *Peru before the Incas*. Englewood Cliffs, New Jersey: Prentice Hall, 1967.

Latour, A. "Velvet." *CIBA Review*, no. 96 (1953): pp. 3438–3463.

Levey, Santina. *Lace: A History*. London: Victoria and Albert Museum, 1985.

Levitt, Sarah. "Registered Designs: New Source Material for the Study of the Mid-Nineteenth Century Fashion Industry." *Costume, The Journal of the Costume Society*, no. 15 (1981): pp. 49–59.

Lucy Truman Aldrich Collection of Japanese Nō Drama Costumes and Priest Robes. Providence, Rhode Island: Art Museum, Rhode Island School of Design, 1937.

MacMillan, Susan L. *Greek Islands Embroideries*. Boston: Museum of Fine Arts, n.d.

Mactaggart, Peter and Ann. "Ease, Convenience and Stays, 1750–1850." *Costume, The Journal of the Costume Society*, 13 (1979): pp. 41–51.

Maeder, Edward. *An Elegant Art: Fact and Fantasy in the Eighteenth Century*. Los Angeles, California: Los Angeles County Museum of Art and New York: Harry N. Abrams, 1983.

Marcoux, Alice. *Jacquard*. Providence, Rhode Island: Museum of Art, Rhode Island School of Design, 1984.

Markowsky, Barbara. *Europäische Seidengewebe des 13.–18. Jahrhunderts*. Cologne: Kunstgewerbemuseum der Stadt Köln, 1976.

Martin, Rebecca. *Textiles in Daily Life in the Middle Ages*. Cleveland, Ohio: The Cleveland Museum of Art, 1985.

Mason, J. Alden. *The Ancient Civilizations of Peru*. Harmondsworth, Middlesex: Penguin Books, 1957.

May, Florence Lewis. *Silk Textiles of Spain: Eighth to Fifteenth Century*. New York: Hispanic Society of America, 1957.

Mayer-Thurman, Christa C. *Raiment for the Lord's Service, A Thousand Years of Western Vestments*. Chicago: Art Institute of Chicago, 1975.

McCardell, Claire. *What Shall I Wear?* New York: Simon and Schuster, 1956.

Meade, Sidney M. *Traditional Maori Clothing*. Auckland: A.H. and A.W. Reed, 1969.

Monnas, Lisa. "Developments in Figured Velvet Weaving in Italy During the 14th Century." *CIETA Bulletin de Liaison*, no. 63–64 (1986): pp. 63–100.

Montgomery, Florence M. *Textiles in America 1650–1870*. New York: W.W. Norton and Co., 1984.

Murra, John V. "Cloth and its Functions in the Inca State." *American Anthropologist*, 64, no. 4 (1962): pp. 710–728.

Museum Notes. Providence, Rhode Island: Museum of Art, Rhode Island School of Design, 1943 to date.

Needler, Winifred. "Three Pieces of Unpatterned Linen From Ancient Egypt in the Royal Ontario Museum." In *Studies in Textile History*, edited by Veronika Gervers. Toronto: Royal Ontario Museum, 1977.

Noma, Seiroku. *Japanese Costume and Textile Arts*. New York: John Weatherhill, 1974.

O'Neale, Lila. "Weaving." *Handbook of South American Indians*. Bulletin 143 of the Bureau of American Ethnology, 5 (1946), pp. 97–137.

Palliser, Mrs. Bury. *History of Lace*. Rev. ed. New York: Charles Scribner's Sons, 1911.

Pareja, Manuel Garcia. *La Industria Sedera en España: El Arte de la Seda de Granada*. Granada: Archivo de la Reale Chancilleria, 1972.

Parslow, Virginia D. "James Alexander, Weaver." *Antiques*, 69, no. 4 (1956), pp. 346–349.

Paul, Ann. "Reestablishing Provenience of Two Paracas Mantles." *Textile Museum Journal*, 4, no. 2 (1975): pp. 30–46.

Petsopoulos, Yanni, ed. *Tulips, Arabesques, and Turbans*. New York: Abbeville Press, 1982.

Pfister, R. *Les Toiles Imprimées de Fostat et de l'Hindoustan*. Paris: Les Éditions d'Art et d'Histoire, 1938.

Picton, John, and John Mack. *African Textiles*. London: British Museum Publications, 1979.

Polychroniadis, Helen. *Greek Embroideries*. Athens: Benaki Museum, 1980.

Prinet, Marguerite. *Le Damas de Lin Historié*. Bern: Fondation Abegg, 1982.

Reath, Nancy Andrews, and Eleanor B. Sachs. *Persian Textiles and their Technique from the Sixth to the Eighteenth Centuries Including a System for General Textile Classification*. New Haven: Yale University Press, 1937.

Ribiero, Aileen. *Dress in Eighteenth-Century Europe 1715–1789*. New York: Holmes and Meier, 1985.

Riefstahl, Rudolf M., "Greek Orthodox Vestments and Ecclesiastical Fabrics." *The Art Bulletin*, 14, no. 4 (1932): pp. 359–373.

Ring, Betty. *Let Virtue be a Guide to Thee*. Providence, Rhode Island: The Rhode Island Historical Society, 1983.

Rodee, Marian E. *Southwestern Weaving*. 2nd ed. Albuquerque: Maxwell Museum of Anthropology and University of New Mexico Press, 1981.

Rogers, J.M., ed. *The Topkapi Saray Museum: Costumes, Embroideries and Textiles*. Boston: Little, Brown, and Company, 1986.

Rothstein, Natalie, ed. *A Lady of Fashion: Barbara Johnson's Album of Styles and Fabrics*. New York: Thames and Hudson, 1987.

Rowe, Ann Pollard. "Technical Features of Inca Tapestry Tunics." *Textile Museum Journal*, 18 (1979): pp. 6–7.

Rowe, Ann Pollard. *Warp Patterned Weaves of the Andes*. Washington, D.C.: Textile Museum, 1977.

Rowe, Ann Pollard. "Weaving Processes of the Cuzco Area of Peru." *Textile Museum Journal*, 4, no. 2 (1975): pp. 30–46.

Rowe, Ann Pollard. "Weaving Styles in the Cuzco Area." In *Ethnographic Textiles in the Western Hemisphere. Irene Emery Roundtable of Museum Textiles, 1976 Proceedings*, edited by Irene Emery and Patricia Fiske. Washington, D.C.: Textile Museum, 1977.

Rowe, John Howland. "Inca Culture at the Time of the Spanish Conquest." *Handbook of South American Indians*. Bulletin 143 of the Bureau of American Ethnology, 4 (1946): pp. 183–330.

Rowe, John Howland. "Standardization in Inca Tapestry Tunics." In *The Junius B. Bird Textile Conference*, edited by Anne Pollard Rowe. Washington, D.C.: Textile Museum, 1979.

Sanday, Peggy R., and Suwati Kartiwa. "Cloth and Custom in West Sumatra." *Expedition*, 26, no. 4 (1984): pp. 13–29.

Sawyer, Alan R. "Paracas and Nazca Iconography." In *Essays in Pre-Columbian Art and Archaeology*, edited by Samuel K. Lothrop. Cambridge, Massachusetts: Harvard University Press, 1961.

Sawyer, Alan R. *Tiahuanaco Tapestry Design*. Studies No. 3. New York: Museum of Primitive Art, 1963.

Scott, A.C. *Chinese Costume in Transition*. Singapore: Donald Moore, 1958.

Serjeant, R.B. *Islamic Textiles: Material for a History up to the Mongol Conquest*. Beirut: Librairie du Liban, 1972.

Shepherd, Dorothy G. "Medieval Persian Silks in Fact and Fancy (A Refutation of the Riggisberg Report)." *CIETA Bulletin de Liaison*, no. 39–40 (1974): pp. 1–239.

Silks from the Palaces of Napoleon. New York: Fashion Institute of Technology, 1983.

Smart, Ellen S. "A Preliminary Report on a Group of Important Mughal Textiles." *Textile Museum Journal*, 25 (1987): pp. 5–23.

Smith, Shea Clark. "Kente Cloth Motifs." *African Arts*, 9, no. 1, (1975): pp. 36–39.

Stearns, Martha Genung. *Home Spun and Blue*. New York: Charles Scribner's Sons, 1940.

Stinchecum, Amanda Mayer. *Kosode: 16th–19th Century Textiles from the Nomura Collection*. New York: Japan Society, 1984.

Stone, Caroline. *The Embroideries of North Africa*. London: Longman Group, 1985.

Swain, Margaret. *The Needlework of Mary Queen of Scots*. New York: Van Nostrand Reinhold, 1973.

Sweeting, C.G. *Combat Flying Clothing*. Washington, D.C.: Smithsonian Institution, 1984.

Thornton, Peter. *Baroque and Rococo Silks*. London: Faber and Faber, 1965.

Thornton, Peter. "The Bizarre Silks." *Burlington Magazine*, 100, no. 665 (1958): pp. 265–270.

Thornton, Peter. *Seventeenth-Century Interior Decoration in England, France, and Holland*. New Haven and London: Yale University, 1978.

Tokyo National Museum. *Noh Play Costume*. Tokyo: Tokyo National Museum, 1987.

Trilling, James. *Aegean Crossroads*. Washington, D.C.: Textile Museum, 1984.

Trilling, James. *The Roman Heritage: Textiles from Egypt and the Eastern Mediterranean 300 to 600 A.D.* Washington, D.C.: Textile Museum, 1982.

Tulokas, Maria. *Textiles for the Eighties*. Providence, Rhode Island: Museum of Art, Rhode Island School of Design, 1985.

Turner, Lucien M. "Ethnology of the Ungava District, Hudson Bay Territory." In *11th Annual Report of the Bureau of Ethnology 1889–90*, edited by J.W. Powell. Washington, D.C.: Government Printing Office, 1894.

Velvets East and West from the 14th to the 20th Century. Los Angeles: Los Angeles County Museum of Art, 1966.

Victoria and Albert Museum. *Rococo Silks*. New York: Harry N. Abrams, 1986.

Vollmer, John. *Decoding Dragons*. Eugene, Oregon: Museum of Art, University of Oregon, 1983.

Vollmer, John. *In the Presence of the Dragon Throne*. Toronto: Royal Ontario Museum, 1977.

Wace, A.J.B. "English Embroideries belonging to Sir John Carew Pole, Bt." *Walpole Society*, 21 (1932–33): pp. 43–65.

Wardwell, Anne. "The Stylistic Development of 14th and 15th Century Italian Silk Design." *Aachener Kunstblätter*, 47 (1976/1977): pp. 177–226.

Warming, Wanda, and Michael Gaworski. *The World of Indonesian Textiles*. Tokyo: Kodansha, 1981.

Weibel, A.C. *Two Thousand Years of Silk Weaving*. New York: n.p., 1944.

Weibel, A.C. *Two Thousand Years of Textiles*. New York: Pantheon, 1952.

Weigert, Roger-Armand. *La Tapisserie et le Tapis en France*. Paris: Presses Universitaires de France, 1964.

Wheat, Joe Ben. "Documentary Basis for Material Changes and Design Styles in Navajo Blanket Weaving." In *Ethnographic Textiles of the Western Hemisphere. Irene Emery Roundtable on Museum Textiles, 1976 Proceedings*, edited by Irene Emery and Patricia Fiske. Washington, D.C.: Textile Museum, 1976.

Wheat, Joe Ben. *The Gift of Spiderwoman. Southwestern Textiles: The Navajo Tradition*. Philadelphia: University Museum, University of Pennsylvania, 1984.

Whitehead, Ruth Holmes. *Micmac Quillwork*. Halifax, Nova Scotia: Nova Scotia Museum, 1982.

Wiet, Gaston. *Soieries Persanes*. Cairo: L'Institut Français d'Archéologie Orientale, 1947.

Willey, Gordon R., ed. *Das Alte Amerika*. Propyläen Kunstgeschichte Bd. 18. Berlin: Propyläen Verlag, 1974.

Wipszycka, Ewa. *L'Industrie Textile dans l'égypte romaine*. Warsaw: Zaklad Narodowy Imienia Osolinskich Wydawnictwo Polskiej Akademii Nauk, 1965.

Woodward, Carla Mathes, and Franklin W. Robinson, eds. *A Handbook of the Museum of Art, Rhode Island School of Design*. Providence, Rhode Island: Museum of Art, Rhode Island School of Design, 1988.

Woven Treasures of Persian Art. Los Angeles: Los Angeles County Museum of Art, 1959.

Yale University Art Gallery. *The Kashmir Shawl*. New Haven: Yale University Art Gallery, 1975.

Zimmern, Nathalie H. "The Tapestries of Colonial Peru." *Brooklyn Museum Journal*, (1943–44): pp. 27–52.

Zimmern, Nathalie H. *Introduction to Peruvian Costume*. New York: The Brooklyn Museum, 1949.

A WORLD OF COSTUME AND TEXTILES
designed by Gilbert Associates
was printed by Meridian Printing
on Bowaters Gleneagle paper.

The type is Aldus, designed for Linotype
in 1952–1953 by Hermann Zapf. It was
named after the 15th century Venetian
printer Aldus Manutius.

The book was bound by Zahrndt's, Inc.

1500 copies for the Museum of Art,
Rhode Island School of Design.

September 1988